The
Cultural Fit
Factor

The Cultural Fit Factor

Creating an Employment Brand

That Attracts, Retains, and Repels

the Right Employees

Lizz Pellet

Society for Human Resource Management
Alexandria, Virginia

This publication is designed to provide accurate and authoritative information regarding the subject matter covered. It is sold with the understanding that neither the publisher nor the author is engaged in rendering legal or other professional service. If legal advice or other expert assistance is required, the services of a competent, licensed professional should be sought. The federal and state laws discussed in this book are subject to frequent revision and interpretation by amendments or judicial revisions that may significantly affect employer or employee rights and obligations. Readers are encouraged to seek legal counsel regarding specific policies and practices in their organizations.

This book is published by the Society for Human Resource Management (SHRM®). The interpretations, conclusions, and recommendations in this book are those of the authors and do not necessarily represent those of the publishers.

The Society for Human Resource Management (SHRM) is the world's largest association devoted to human resource management. Representing more than 250,000 members in over 140 countries, the Society serves the needs of HR professionals and advances the interests of the HR profession. Founded in 1948, SHRM has more than 575 affiliated chapters within the United States and subsidiary offices in China and India. Visit SHRM Online at www.shrm.org.

Interior and Cover Design: Shirley E.M. Raybuck

Library of Congress Cataloging-in-Publication Data

Pellet, Lizz.
   The cultural fit factor : creating an employment brand that attracts, retains, and repels the right employees / Lizz Pellet.
       p. cm.
   Includes bibliographical references and index.
   ISBN 978-1-58644-126-5
   1. Employees—Recruiting. 2. Employee selection. 3. Corporate culture. 4. Branding (Marketing) 5. Personnel management. I. Title.
   HF5549.5.R44P454 2009
   658.3'01—dc22

                                    2009017678

10 9 8 7 6 5 4   14-0528

Contents

Acknowledgments

They say it takes a village to raise a child to which, I humbly add, it takes a tribe to write a good business book. It is never one person's voice or research that makes a great body of work. Conversations, stories, data, studies and articles give authors the fodder to build on and create new thoughts. I would like to thank my tribe.

There are some incredible conference directors and program coordinators in our midst. They are the ones that seek out new ideas, schools of thought, and great speakers. They know that while the setting and often times the food are a memorable experience, the speakers and educators are what attendees remember and come back to see and hear year after year. Anna Brekka and Laura Tremblay from Kennedy Information, R.D. Whitney from Onrec, Susan Frear from the Dallas Human Resource Management Association, Scott Sundy from ADVANCE Newsmagazines, Todd Raphael from ERE, Ron Goode from the American Staffing Association, Barry Asin from Staffing Industry Analysts, Debbie McGrath from HR.com and Braden Albert from HR Star are all visionaries and leaders in this category.

With so many professional associations that send out a call for presenters, it is the volunteer selection committees who process hundreds of speaker requests. They are the stewards of securing top speaking talent and fresh content. To all of these associations and committees that have chosen me to speak over the years, I have been honored and offer a heartfelt thanks.

Thank you to the researchers, writers, bloggers and tweeters who have provided incredible (and reliable) research, data, and studies. I appreciate your commitment to the profession and sharing this information.

My friends and colleagues who have taken the time to review the content of this book, suggest, critique, and laugh out loud, I give you my sincere thanks and gratitude. There are many industry professionals who I bounced this information. They would have loved to contribute their feedback and endorsements — but like culture suggests, sometimes organizations are bound by the knots of legal departments and constraints of PR. That is not a bad thing, as you will read in this book, sometimes it just is what it is.

I would like to thank Maureen Henson, SPHR, president of R&M Associates, and Dr. Michael R. Kannisto, vice president, Staffing/University Relations/Employment Branding, BASF Corporation, for reviewing earlier versions of the manuscript.

And lastly, my thanks to SHRM and the great staff for working with me through this process.

Dedication

To Reagan Forlenzo, Om Mani Phat Me Hum. This book would have never been written without your dedication and support.

To Andrew Fortham and Madelyn Fortham, you can be anything you want to be, you just have to try.

To those on the path: Truly, the greatest gift you have to give is that of your own self-transformation.

Lao Tzu.

And finally, to Ralph the Hamster — thanks for keeping the wheel going, even after hours.

CHAPTER 1

The Foundation for Integrating Organizational Culture and the Employment Brand

"The man in black fled across the desert, and the gunslinger followed."

That's the opening line to Stephen King's magnum opus, *The Dark Tower* series,[1] a seven-book series composed of nearly 4,000 pages, which took King more than two decades to complete. Why is the master of horror's work so fascinating that it should be used in the opening of a Human Resources book? It's all about the journey.

The main character, Roland, starts his epic adventure, which takes him through an experience of many trials and tribulations — love, landscape, loss, wonderment, adventure, danger, and, ultimately, the understanding of how difficult and triumphant values and the human spirit can be. The most fascinating piece of this epic tale is the culmination of Roland's quest, his journey, and his life's work. He reaches his final destination and finds the Dark Tower. He ascends the long staircase, identifies his final triumph, opens the door … and the story ends the way it began: "The man in black fled across the desert, and the gunslinger followed."

How many times in our professional lives do we seek the pinnacle of our career, the job of jobs, only to discover that it wasn't what we thought it would be, that we don't really *fit*, and it really isn't the Holy Grail we've been searching for? That's the premise of this book. The cultural *fit* factor — how we can find the right *fit* in our professional experience; how the strategic thinkers in Human Resources can find the people who will *fit* in their organizations and have the ultimate authentic and congruent work experience; and how we can create an employment brand that will convey the real culture of the organization.

I've been assessing organizational culture for almost 15 years. In that time, I have seen a significant number of organizations with healthy cultures, some that are moderately healthy, and some that are unhealthy, yet successful. I noticed a trend emerging: Organizations with healthy cultures really know who they are. Their employees have a sense of belonging, identity, and *esprit de corps*. It's much like how the book *Built to Last* so prophetically pointed out that there is a "cult-like culture" within these organizations.[2]

So, naturally, I was intrigued by these cultures. Was this a "Stepford Wife" situation in which the corporation stocks itself with pliant androids, perfect beyond belief? Had Human Resources moved down into the basement, far behind the boilers, offering up the same employee in a different skin, over and over again? Or have these organizations really banded together, honoring diversity, creating a sense of community and elitism above their competitors in today's war for talent?

It became time to infuse a new element into my approach for assessing organizational culture. By weaving in questions about employment branding, I could get a better sense of whether the organizations with healthy cultures also had created a significant employment brand.

I set out to learn more about branding, from various perspectives: recruitment advertising, marketing, consumer packaging, and companies that have well-known brands. I needed to learn more about branding so that I could incorporate branding concepts, philosophies, and methodologies into the cultural diagnostic process I had already developed.

Organizational Diagnosis Process: The performance objective represents the process' ability to guide organizational adaptability, stability, and innovation.

Structure. Division of Labor, Departmentalization, and Organizational Type

Strategy. Business Definition, Success Factors, Competitive Analysis, Business Plan, Succession Planning

Tasks. Skill Requirements and Competence

Decision Support Systems. Planning, Control, and Budgeting Information

Human Resource Systems. Demographics, Skills, Motives, Expectations, Recruitment-Selection, and Training and Development

Reward Systems. Compensation, Promotions, and Opportunities for Advancement as the Primary Source for Understanding Organizational Performance Outputs.

I examined cultural assessment findings in a new way — from an employment-branding perspective. As I reviewed client report data, I thought that *if* I was an employee of this company, would these results attract me to work at this company; get even the passive candidates to find interest in the company; retain me as a current employee; encourage me to stay employed by this company; or repel me altogether?

So, for the last few years, I've been talking about the Attract, Retain, and Repel concept. Sure, everyone understands the concept of attract and retain ... but repel? Isn't "repel" a dirty word?

Now, I've heard many HR professionals say, "We want to invite *everyone* to apply! We don't want to exclude anyone!" and "We have to let everyone apply; we are a union shop. Our doors are always open, and anyone who thinks we are not in compliance with EEOC can check our records." These may be true statements, but do you really want *everyone* to apply? These are the folks who, in *Good to Great*, say, "We have to have everyone on the same bus."[3] But you don't want some candidates to even know you *have* a bus! Think about it. There are employees in every company who really just don't fit. You know who I'm talking about. The ones who you wish you could gather around the water cooler and then bring in Jeff Probst from "Survivor" to say, "George, the tribe has spoken. It's time for you to go." And, poof, out goes the torch and they exit the organization.

And it's never the same *type* of person for every company because every organization has a different culture. The employee who sticks out like a sore thumb in Company A fits seamlessly in Company B. So the real goal here is to repel the employees who just don't fit from even *applying* at Company A in the first place. It would be much more economical if they just submitted their resume right over to Company B. That's the beauty of a clear and definitive employment brand in the context of repel.

Replacement Costs

We all know what it can mean when you're not clear on your employment brand or candidate expectations — everybody comes in to apply for a job. Your recruiter's time and energy turns from a strategic placement specialist into a resume sorter. Retention is always important because of the investment you make in people. While people investments are different from one industry to the next — and greater from employer to employer — everyone can agree that the costs are great. You've heard the statistics of a bad hire, right? Statistics from the U.S. Department of Labor reveal that the average cost to replace a worker in the private industry is $13,996.[4] In 2007, they show an estimated cost of a single vacancy for some jobs was calculated to cost anywhere from $7,000 to $12,000 per day. In

2006, Salary.com reported replacement cost ranging from nearly 29 percent of an employee's annual wages. How's that for the potential cost of high turnover?

It is estimated that one out of every four employees has been with their company less than one year. *Less than one year?* It takes 90 days to find your way around and gain entry into the intact social circles. Factor in another 90 days to figure out the 4 P's (process, procedures, protocol, and politics), and you have about four months of steady and reliable productivity from one in every four workers in your company. And that's frightening, especially if you're a recruiter.

Why do we continue to put the new hires through this meat-grinder process and weigh down our already overworked employees with the responsibility of being mentors, preceptors, buddies, or tour guides only to repeat the cycle of onboarding employees who really don't fit into the culture *in the first place*!

The bottom line with Attract, Retain, and Repel is that when you understand and *embrace* who you are and who you are not, as an organization, you will attract and retain the *right* employees and repel the ones who just won't fit. By incorporating this concept and repelling employees who don't fit into your culture, you reduce recruitment expenses significantly.[5]

CHAPTER 2
So What *Is* Organizational Culture?

Organizational culture has its theoretical origins in sociology and anthropology. These sciences are critical in helping us to understand societal groups. They also help us understand why people act the way they do, because culture has a significant effect on human behavior.

Culture is defined as a set of beliefs, values, customs, and behaviors that members of a society use to relate to their world and each other. It is also defined as the norms that we live by — the commonly held meanings and actions for a specific human gathering. In many respects, our values and beliefs are determinants of our behavior.

Unspoken Rules

As a member of a culture, you learn that when you behave outside of what is considered acceptable or legal, there is a consequence that often involves a sanction or punishment. Although the threat of an unpleasant outcome serves as a deterrent to inappropriate behaviors for many, people in every society break the rules to some extent. Tolerance of actions that fall outside of the cultural expectations seems to vary with the number of people who violate those expectations. For example, when you're driving in a clearly posted 45-mph speed zone at 45 mph, but everyone is passing you, suddenly you notice that your speedometer is showing 51 mph and it seems reasonable. In fact, once you start going 51 mph and pass someone going the speed limit, you may even think there's something wrong with the other driver's behavior! The outcome in this case, a speeding ticket, is not universally applied because the police can only catch and ticket a fraction of the people who are speeding. In time, the posted speed limit might actually be changed, or speeders will be ignored.

The beliefs, values, and behaviors that are a part of an organization affect the individuals in that organization, the product or service that organization provides, and the organization as a whole. There seems to be an inability to define culture, which leads to a high level of frustration for you as a leader. How are you expected to manage something that you can't always identify or define, let alone measure? When I started assessing culture, it was as elusive to me as trying to nail Jell-O to the wall.

Often, there are subcultures within your overarching organizational culture. Stop perpetuating *the same old way of doing things;* rather than managing these two worlds, you must strive to eliminate the unspoken, hidden culture. The answer is not to learn how to manage the unspoken culture, but to eliminate it. Why? Because living under both the spoken and unspoken law gets confusing for your workforce, and it gets in the way of achieving profitable results.

The good news is that conducting a cultural assessment allows you to examine these two worlds. You will be able to identify what your unspoken assumptions are and learn how you can create the right type of structure to combine these two worlds, the hidden and the overt, and ultimately eliminate your hidden culture (see Table 2.1).

The concept of organizational culture needs to be simplified. A cultural assessment is the only vehicle that can help you reach that understanding. When conducting an assessment, examine what the unspoken assumptions are, why they exist, and how you work with them. The double standards that you continue to perpetuate in your business must stop. What you say on paper must reflect how you act and vice versa. Your words must equal your actions.

What Is the Cultural Health Indicator™ (CHI)?

This assessment tool was developed in 1999. It is one of the key assessment tools and, most often, the first step in the cultural due diligence process. The CHI is a validated, diagnostic instrument that focuses on the need for identifying organizational balance and alignment. The process of alignment and balance is what we term "congruence." Theoretically, management and organizational philosophies have focused on the critical changes necessary to enhance organizational structure, organizational operational processes, organizational environments, and organizational policies and procedures. The focus of these philosophies has been one-sided. The forgotten side often has been the human component of the organization. When dysfunction or frustration begins to develop, it is the human component that is most impacted, and it is the human component that is most misunderstood and forgotten. This instrument therefore looks at the health of an organization based on its balance and alignment of people and system issues. The instrument focuses on the governing principles, formal organizational systems, informal organizational systems, organizational characteristics, and organizational values that frame the direction and actions of organizations. It is not what the organization believes exists that drives the effectiveness of the organization's action; it is the perception and, ultimately, the actions or nonactions of the employees at all levels of the organization that determine the health of the organization.

Table 2.1. What a Cultural Assessment Should Measure

Below are the cultural dimensions examined by the EMERGE International Brand Enhancer and Cultural Health Indicator™ assessment tools. These tools were created in 2000 and have been deployed to more than 250 organizations.

Identity	☐ Knowledge of brand ☐ Emotional connection to brand ☐ Brand identity
Leadership	☐ Vision, mission, values ☐ Business strategy development ☐ Leadership effectiveness ☐ Ethics
Relationships	☐ Trust ☐ Collaboration ☐ Inter/Intra group relationships ☐ Community ☐ Customers
Communication	☐ Feedback ☐ Information sharing ☐ Employee trust in information
Infrastructure	☐ Formal procedures ☐ Processes, systems, policies, and structure ☐ Teams
Involvement & Decision-Making	☐ Authority levels ☐ Accountability and expectations ☐ Decision-making process ☐ Empowerment
Employee Engagement	☐ Creativity and innovation ☐ Recognition ☐ Continuous learning ☐ Diversity
Finance	☐ Perception of financial health and the role of the employee in profitability ☐ Level of financial comprehension and individual impact on the business
Cultural Descriptors	☐ Validate stated values congruence with real experience. The employees are asked what values they would like to experience and then they are asked what values they currently experience. This provides an immediate gap analysis.
General Climate	☐ Qualitative: open-ended questions that capture the stories and suggestions from employees. This step allows the stories to support the quantitative data you have collected and negates the need for conducting focus groups.

If It Is Broken, Fix It

Let's work with some concrete examples from some of the dimensions you can measure. You have a company policy that clearly outlines how RFPs are processed. However, in talking with employees, you discover that they haven't followed that procedure for years. Why? Because it's cumbersome and their reaction is *we'd never get anything done if we followed it.* Or, you have an HR policy that states that all positions will be posted internally before going to the outside. Yet, many people know that a number of positions were filled that were never posted, or, worse yet, positions were posted after the external recruiting process had begun. These are blatant incongruencies between formal and informal policies, between the stated way of getting things done and the way things really get done. These incongruencies not only cause confusion in the eyes of your employees, but they also cause high levels of frustration and anger, and begin to eat away at your trust level.

So what does this have to do with bottom-line results? Excluding culture from your calculations is like ignoring warning signs you get from your doctor. Culture tells you *how* you are achieving your results, positive or negative. It tells you why you're in the red or why you're in the black. When you have a healthy bottom line and healthy profit margins, there is no reason to examine *how* you are achieving such great results. Or is that really true? If you don't have a basic understanding of how you achieve your results, then it becomes virtually impossible to replicate what is working and modify what is not working. Baselines must be established for any and all processes that you use in your day-to-day operations, and your cultural process is no exception. If you don't understand what *is* and *is not* working from a quantifiable perspective, you will just be shooting in the dark. And you know that as rapidly as businesses are moving today, you must be able to hit the target on the first try, by knowing what the target is and where it is.

A significant driver in fixing broken processes or transforming an unhealthy culture is that organizational culture is the foundation that supports profitability (see Figure 2.1). The ability of an organization to deliver on its strategic objectives depends largely on the employees' performance. There are hundreds of publications on employee satisfaction and energy levels, and the effect on productivity. The "happier" or more satisfied an individual is, the more they are willing to "give" or produce. If the right processes, products, resources, and support mechanisms are in place, satisfied employees deliver and have an energy level that allows them to meet objectives. We could also agree that having those processes, products, resources, and support mechanisms in place, or not having them in place, also speaks to the level of health of the organizational culture. Satisfied employees give off this positive energy, which manifests into higher levels of care for the organization, and which creates increased quality of products and, often, increased customer satisfaction levels. This all drives revenues, which drives earnings — and stakeholder value. Keep in mind, there are many external forces that can inhibit an organization from having a high level of employee satisfaction. The factors that can significantly affect the organizational culture, which has an impact on employee satisfaction are:[1]

- No Structured Process for Change
- Senior Management Turnover
- Lack of a Clear Vision and Mission
- Uncertain Economy
- Lack of Involvement
- Management Behaviors
- Confusing Leadership Messages
- Increasing Workloads
- Lack of Accountability
- Unclear Career Paths
- Poor Communication
- Layoffs
- Tension
- Restructuring
- New Strategy
- Mergers
- Acquisitions
- Lack of Trust
- Ethics
- Competing Agendas

Organizational culture can be referred to as the glue that keeps an organization together. It is the silent code of conduct; it's more about *how* things get done, rather than *what* gets done. It can also be referred to as white noise, the background static that may affect you but goes unnoticed. When new employees are *learning the ropes*, they are learning the culture.

Culture is not a thing. It's not something an organization has or doesn't have. Culture is something an organization *is*. Your organization could be assessed today, and you would be able to define your culture in specific terms and even identify subcultures. The challenge for you, as a leader, is to recognize that it exists and that it molds reality for your employees. Your job is to ensure that the culture does not become dysfunctional. When this happens, culture, especially if it's a strong one, can be a liability. A cultural assessment allows you to continuously examine your culture and to determine how healthy it is. It will identify where your incongruencies lie,

Figure 2.1 Organizational Culture and Impact on Earnings

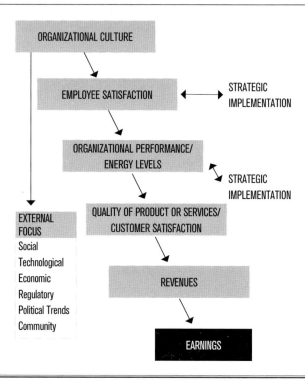

Source: EMERGE International, 2002

determine what effect they are having on your business, and help you develop a plan to rectify the situation.

Culture has many different characteristics that can affect its degree of influence on members of the group. One of my favorite culture books, *Built to Last*,[2] was the first business book to talk about *cult-like cultures* and their effect on visionary (a.k.a. successful) companies.

Not many companies being created today believe that their core foundation and ideology is what will make them successful in the future. You remember the dot.com era, right? Right, foundation — what foundation? Many companies are built on an idea, technology, and/or fad that just might come and go. And when those do "go" (and more often than not they do), the company goes as well. Organizations that have realized and recognized that they must start with a solid foundation and vision and stick with it tend to *last*.

The organizational cultures the authors of *Built to Last* refer to are almost cult-like. All of the examples come from "visionary companies," which the authors define as premier institutions in their industries, widely admired by their peers, and having a long track record of success. Although they caution that "we're not saying that visionary companies are cults," they suggest that some of these companies use techniques that might be found in cults. Specifically, they found that some of the visionary companies:

- Had a lengthy indoctrination to company policy and procedure. Example: Disney's requirement that every new employee attend Disney University.
- Demonstrated a "greater tightness of fit." Employees either buy in or get out. Example: Nordstrom is recognized for its commitment to outstanding customer service, and it is reported that 50 percent of new hires leave because they just don't fit into the organization. The employees that stay are referred to as "Nordies."
- Showed more elitism. Example: Companies like Nike and the U.S. Marines.

Do you know anyone who has your company logo tattooed on their body? Yes, you read that correctly. If your answer was "no," then evidently you don't know one of the many diehards who work for Nike. It's not unusual for Nike employees to get the Nike swoosh tattooed below the knee on their left leg (the lead leg for most runners in the starting block).

What about the U.S. Marine Corps? Elitism to the core: *Semper Fidelis* isn't just their motto, it's a way of life. It guides Marines to remain faithful to the mission at hand, to each other, to the Corps, and to country, no matter what. Becoming a Marine is a transformation that cannot be undone, and *Semper Fi* reminds us of that. Once made, a Marine will forever live by the ethics and values of the Corps. There is no such thing as an ex-Marine.[3] That's an undeniably powerful statement.

Case in Point: The Mayo Clinic

This case describes my experience with an elitist culture. The Mayo Clinic views itself as a premier health care provider and employer. The Mayo way of doing things is part of a culture that has been sustained for more than a century. It starts with their mission, the organizational mantra "the best interest of the patient is the only interest to be considered." This mantra has become a standard against which every decision is measured and has made Mayo a premier healthcare provider, especially in the eyes of the patient.

After spending nine months with the Mayo Clinic-Scottsdale developing and implementing the education and orientation plan for their new hospital in Arizona, I can attest to that strong culture. From the day I came through the front door, I could feel lots of energy, a positive charge that hummed throughout the building. Some of the old-timers told me that as an outsider I would have to be Mayo-ized in order to be accepted in the system. They were right. I became Mayo-ized, and I quickly discovered that all the employees had, too. From the Chief Nursing Officer to the Environmental Services Tech, whenever I asked an employee to recite the mission of the Mayo Clinic, they would look me straight in the eyes and say, "The best interest of the patient is the only interest to be considered." "How do you know that?" I'd ask. "You didn't even have to turn your badge over!" "I don't know – I just do!" would inevitably be their response. They had become Mayo-ized and didn't even know it. I also found their onboarding programs to be exacting: On the first day, employees learn about the mission, and that is supported through the entire employee experience. This process and commitment translates into profit as well.

It may have started out as a small outpatient facility, but now, a century later, the Mayo Clinic is one of the top-ranked hospitals in the nation, with annual revenues of nearly $7 billion. The Mayo Clinic does something really well that any medium size or larger company can do better: the pooling of talent. You find the right kind of people, and then create a culture in which they work harder than most people. It's the power of culture, the power of teamwork, the power of a legacy; it makes people proud. If you are really proud of your organization, you work harder for it.[4] I certainly found this to be true. Employees were evaluated not only on their technical skill and experience, but also on how fully they adopted and applied the Mayo mission, vision, and philosophy in their work. It's about aptitude and attitude.

Culture and a Common Understanding

I define organizational culture as the mechanism that truly defines the organization for the employees and the customers: how things really get done, how people interact with each other. Organizational culture represents a common understanding held by all employees. It is a system of shared meaning. This guiding culture expresses the core organizational values that must be shared by the entire employee population. In addition to this guiding culture, large organizations will have many subcultures (departments or divisions). These subcultures typically reflect common problems, situations, or experiences that affect members of that particular department or division. This doesn't mean that the subcultures supplant the guiding culture. However, keeping them from supplanting the guiding culture is the challenge of many organizations today. When subcultures are not connected to the guiding culture, there is a disconnect, which can cause confusion for an employee, especially in a divisional transfer situation.

The guiding culture should be what governs the behavior of every employee. It should embody the core organizational values that all employees must live by. The subcultures should be merely an adjunct to the macro culture.

The guiding culture (or core organizational values) is wholesome and full of integrity. This will be the case when the guiding culture is defined by all levels in an organization, and not just by the people who live in the ivory tower. The guiding culture tells you, as a new employee, what is expected, even if all that's expected is that the bottom line comes before ethics. In this situation, a new employee has to decide whether he or she wants to work for such an organization. The employee has to make a clear choice, and that's the important point. The guiding culture's rules and expectations, whatever they are, should be clear, congruent, and apply to everyone, so that employees will know where they stand and how to act on the company's behalf.

Along with these definitions come key determinants that contribute to and define organizational culture. Deploying a cultural assessment will enable you to examine these key determinants in a comprehensive, structured approach. They should include:

- *Physical Layout*. Do private offices exist? If so, who has them? Are there offices or conference rooms set up as think tanks, or are the departments filled with floor-to-ceiling cubicles?
- *Interactions*. How do employees get along with each other, with customers, and with vendors? How do they communicate with each other?
- *Language*. Is there a common language? What is the jargon that is used? What about acronyms? How are people addressed? Are formal titles used?
- *Dress*. Is there a formal or informal dress code?
- *Rules of the Game*. How do things really get done around here? This is important for newcomers.
- *Group Norms*. What is acceptable practice? Is it the norm to arrive 15 minutes late to a meeting? Do people rationalize that lateness by saying, "That's OK! Our watches are set on (fill in your company's name) time"?

- *Values.* What are they and how are they practiced?
- *Relationships.* How does the board interact with the CEO and vice versa? How does the workforce as a whole interact? How many people actually showed up to the last company social outing/gathering?
- *Self-image.* Tough or caring? Environmentally responsible?
- *Structure.* Is the organization hierarchical, matrixed, or boundaryless?
- *Process.* How do decisions get made?
- *Leadership.* Do you have a formal or informal leadership structure?

Culture and People Practices

Human behavior has a direct and measurable impact on the performance levels of an organization. Think about this for a minute. How many of the tasks within your organization can be accomplished without human interaction or human dependency? Yes, one could argue that we are in a technological age, where human interaction, once the mainstay of the manufacturing floor, has been replaced by robots and automated plants. We may think that since we're doing work via such high-tech media as the Internet that there is less human interaction. However, this technology has not and will never eliminate the human interactions that must take place in conducting business. Look more closely. Is the task of building a car in a robot plant accomplished by the robot or is it accomplished by the people who designed the robot or program? Crucial human interaction was involved there. In addition, although we may be sitting in front of our computer alone as we use the Internet, we use it primarily for communication, which is definitely human interaction. Sure, transactions do occur in a "virtual" environment more often today than ever before, but there is still a human behind the machine. The way we convey our messages across telephone lines is just as critical as a face-to-face encounter, and face-to-face encounters have not been eliminated, by any means. Skype has enhanced the global face-to-face interaction via the Internet and webcams. The people who are left on the manufacturing floor these days must still interact with each other in order to get their jobs done. Employees from one department in a hospital must coordinate their efforts with other departments to deliver the best possible patient care. The bottom line is that humans will always be required to interact with each other at some level.

You must pay attention to culture and the people factor (your human capital), because, with the dizzying pace of change in business, people know that they are expendable; they don't have the loyalty and allegiance to their employers that employees a generation ago might have had. This is a big cultural shift. A lifetime career with a single organization is nearly unheard of today. The increase in job changing has become a fact of life that affects organizations. I'm sure that you can personally attest to the high cost of recruitment, retention, and replacement.

However, these costs represent just part of the value of human capital. To illustrate the point, consider the often-told story about the tourist who approached Pablo Picasso as he was sketching in a Paris café. The tourist asked Picasso to paint her portrait, which the artist agreed to do and quickly completed. When the tourist asked what she owed, Picasso told her 5,000 francs, which was much more than she expected. "But it only took you a few minutes," she protested. "No," said Picasso, "It took me all my life." She, like so many of us, failed to consider the value associated with lifelong commitment and experience. Not taking Picasso's attitude toward the value of human capital today can lead to missed opportunities to leverage precious intellectual capital.

More than ever before, you must recognize the value of your people and the hand they play in creating your organization's culture and wealth. In *Intellectual Capital*, author Annie Brooking suggests that "every time we lose an employee we lose a chunk of corporate memory."[5] Her research confirms the importance of finding and keeping employees with knowledge and experience. Yet, according to Brooking, "lost expertise is a huge problem few companies have attempted to solve." If you don't pay attention to this part of your culture, your brainpower (or knowledge asset) will go elsewhere.

This scenario occurs frequently, especially in the communications and technology sectors. No one can argue, from a brand point of view, that Bill Gates is Microsoft or Warren Buffet is Berkshire Hathaway. What would happen if these people suddenly left and joined the competition? Many organizations guard against that possibility with contract clauses that prohibit certain executives and knowledge workers from immediately going to work for the direct competition. Such a loss of intellectual capital would be devastating to the organization and the bottom line. People really do make or break the profits. The corporate line that we are all expendable — replaceable — may be fiction, and it may actually damage the corporate culture. On the flip side, when the CEO is the brand, and falls from grace, it can have a negative impact on the bottom line. The bigger the name is, the bigger the need to manage that image to keep the company value high.

It is important for companies to know where they are in the life cycle of their business so they can know when to make changes. If you and your company are not constantly improving performance levels, your organization will begin to lose ground. However, many companies, when reaching the point where changes must be made, fail to realize that they cannot reach the next performance level without people, without human capital. How many of us have rebuilt, resized, restructured, re-engineered, and reorganized our companies to meet the many challenges of the global marketplace? Work processes have been adapted to improve productivity and increase shareholder value. We have fixed the hard stuff. However, many of us are beginning to recognize that, in order to get to the next level of performance, we must focus on the soft stuff. We must deal with the toughest issue, our people, and, inevitably, our organizational culture. The soft stuff really is the hard stuff.

Culture and Procedural Practices

Actions translate into the story that is told. People then make assumptions from the story. Change the story, and you change the assumptions! Changing the assumptions changes people's behavior and therefore changes the culture, plain and simple. It comes down to behavior and how we practice that behavior.

When we talk about practice in culture, we are talking about the way that the values are translated into accepted standards of practice. These are the policies and procedures that, loosely translated, become the "bible" for organizations. But as we all know, the Bible can be interpreted both literally and figuratively. One person's take on a specific scripture can be almost the total opposite of another person's. It is the same in your organization. You have the literal interpretation of the policy that states employees are not permitted to eat at their work stations, but you have the unwritten rule that says it is OK if there are no clients who can see them and if they do it without making a mess. These unwritten assumptions represent the hidden culture.

You may have a cohabitation or anti-nepotism policy that states that two people cannot work in the same department if they live together, especially if one is a supervisor, but everybody knows a "real nice couple" in the same department. They're breaking the policy, but you look the other way. Once you start to think about it, you may find the list of official policies and procedures that vary from the real practice in your organization is longer than you imagined. These are examples of incongruencies in your organization that, over time, slowly eat away at your company's values and, ultimately, your culture. In the context of employment branding, your values will need to be clearly communicated in the brand messaging and be congruent with the actual work experience.

CHAPTER 3

Employment Branding and the Employee Value Proposition

In 2006, when I began my quest for information on employment branding, there were far too few articles that specifically linked employment brand to organizational culture. Most of the research explained brand from a marketing- or consumer-branding perspective. Any time I asked a dozen people what brand meant to them, they gave me a dozen different answers.

The definitions of employment brand were so different that it was difficult to arrive at common understanding of the concept. A common response in our employment branding study (see Appendix A) was that one of the most difficult things for participants was "selling branding" to their executives (due to the inability to clearly define branding and communicate the ROI of the effort).

To me, an employment brand is the articulation of your company culture and the true message of what's it like to work there. It is a carefully crafted message, which can be delivered in several modalities, and it is both authentic and congruent. It is the bases of the reality of the employee experience and it can be spread virally through technology, dialogue, and employee interaction. This viral approach is why the brand must be authentic and congruent; employees can spread negative news about the organization as easily as they can spread the positive news. An employment brand is aligned with your consumer brand, but is not one and the same. The significance of your brand to new hires and current employees must be able to be measured and tracked via onboarding surveys or employee opinion polls. Simply stated, employees need to know what it is so that you can substantiate the ROI of the branding effort. Finally, it must be clear — so clear that the individual has an intuitive reaction to whether he or she would be a good "fit" or not. Clarity of message is important as it will attract some candidates, retain the employees who do find a real experience, and easily repel a candidate from applying in the first place. It should conjure up a "bitter face" for the prospective employee who would never "fit in."

Definitions, Ideas, and Thoughts from the Experts

As my research for a definition concluded, I found that there were several different perspectives on what brand is and is not. I want to share them with you so you will have a choice in creating your own organization's definition of the employment brand.

Robert Rodrigues offers the following definition:

> An employment brand is an image an organization conveys as to what it is like to work there. The brand provides an expression of the attributes that characterizes the employers' work experience and in essence provides a window into what it's like to work in and for the organization.[1]

An *HR Solutions* article stated:

> Employer branding reflects an organization's intentional strategy to create a specific perception of employment at the company. It is the projection of a certain image as an employer. Branding is important for companies that desire a competitive edge in recruitment and employee retention. In addition, it helps to define corporate culture, cultivate company values and strategically deliver an organization's message.[2]

This definition suggests that branding helps define corporate culture. I think they have it backwards: Culture should define brand, not vice versa.

The American Marketing Association defines brand as a "name, term, sign, symbol or design, or a combination of them, intended to identify the goods and services of one seller or group of sellers to differentiate them from those of the competition."[3] Unfortunately, this doesn't translate easily into employment branding.

A large recruitment-advertising firm gave the following definition in an article on their web site and left me feeling like I was playing buzzword bingo:

> Employment branding is a long-term strategy that helps create the right perception of your unique employment experience and cultivate meaningful connections with talent. While the focus of employment branding is often external communications, employment brand strategy is most effective when it connects with talent consistently, at every phase of the employee lifecycle. While the trend toward an increasingly competitive labor market creates challenges in attracting quality talent, it also means new opportunities for the best players on our current roster. And that makes engagement and retention mission-critical to the future success of the enterprise.[4]

There are also definitions from some of the online job boards that offer branding services. Here is what CareerBuilder.com states:

> Employment branding is the process of placing an image of being a great place to work in the minds of the targeted talent pool. When you implement these tools into your recruiting efforts, you effectively create an image that makes people want to work for your company. Regardless of how you wish for job seekers to view your company, employment branding helps you project that image successfully.[5]

Unfortunately after the definition, they do not help you determine what the image should be or help you to create it into a succinct and successful message. You have to buy their Brandbuilder tool for that.

A Business Case for Branding

Regardless of whether or not a precise definition can be agreed upon, there are distinct benefits derived from creating an employment brand and rolling it into a message for the entire world to see and hear. John Sullivan, a widely quoted expert on HR practices, states it correctly:

> … the primary reason why corporate recruiting managers under appreciate and under utilize a corporate branding strategy is because they have done a poor job in making the business case for investing in their firm's employment brand. You can't make a compelling business case unless you first know the possible benefits of the branding strategy.[6]

The business case is crucial here. Getting the C-suite to pay attention to this process and invest in it may be the first step in the creation of a successful brand. For many of these senior-level executives, it's all about charts and graphs — quantitative data that shows ROI. For this reason alone, the importance of creating something you can measure is paramount.

Sullivan outlines the benefits of having an employment branding program. They are:

- A long-term impact — five years (baring any negative PR issues with the company)
- An increased volume of unsolicited candidates
- Higher-quality candidates
- Higher offer-acceptance ratios
- Increased employee referrals

- Improved employee retention rates
- Increased employee motivation
- Improved college recruitment
- A stronger corporate culture
- Decreased corporate negatives
- Ammunition for employees and managers
- Increased manager satisfaction
- Increased media exposure
- A competitive advantage
- Increased shareholder value
- Support for the product brand

Many of these outcomes will resurface in some of the examples and stories about companies that are creating employment brands to attract, retain, and, yes, even repel to increase the ROI of recruitment and retention.

The Employee Value Proposition

If we define employment branding as the articulation of the employment experience and the Employee Value Proposition (EVP), then we need to understand what EVP is all about. The business community talks about the value proposition of products or services, the buy. The buy can be two-sided: (1) What we are purchasing for our company and (2) what the consumer is going to buy from us. It doesn't matter if this is a business-to-business purchase or a direct consumer purchase, the discussion centers around the value of that purchase — and our return on that purchase.

The same can be said for the EVP. Organizations provide something that (1) prospective and current employees "buy into" and (2) what the organization expects to get "paid back." Simply stated, it's what the organization is going to give, what the employee is going to get, and in turn, give back.

I have found companies that have combined a rebranding effort to support both their consumer organizations and employment brand. Many of them were large companies, but that doesn't mean smaller companies cannot or should not follow suit. Liberty Mutual, Con-way, Whirlpool, and Procter & Gamble have all gone through a major rebranding effort. They have transformed their consumer brands as well as leveraged their employee value propositions to create a competitive and sustainable brand. They have clearly differentiated themselves in the minds of the consumer and potential employee. We will look at their approaches and outcomes as examples throughout this chapter.

EVP is all about what the company is willing to give and what the employee is going to get. When you're creating a brand, you need to take all the components of your EVP, start with a broad overview of what you're going to give, and then be able to define what the employee is going to get.

Today's employee wants more than a job. People are now seeking a work experience. They have more of a vision around what they're looking for than in past decades. They see a bigger picture.

This vision of a work experience rather than just a job reminds me of the age-old parable about two men laboring in the hot sun in medieval Italy. They were both dripping with sweat, their muscles straining as they chiseled huge blocks of marble. A priest walked by and asked one man, "What are you doing, my son?" His faced was downcast, and without looking up, he replied, "I am chipping stone." The priest looked at the other man who, while still straining and sweating, wore an exultant smile on his face and his eyes were alight with passion. "And what are you doing, my son?" the priest asked him. "I am building a cathedral!" he answered. These two workers were looking at the same thing, doing the same work, but one saw only what was in front of him and the other had incredible vision.

There is a trend toward creating more emotional employment branding messages. They are created to grab both the head and the heart of potential employees. Liberty Mutual Insurance is a great example of the emotional shift; they have created it in both the external and internal brand.

Case Overview: Liberty Mutual

Liberty Mutual has recently created one of the more compelling brands that I have experienced. The first time I came across the new brand, I was watching television and saw their new commercial (or branding campaign). The first thing that grabbed me was the music, as it was very compelling. I watched the entire 60-second commercial and something struck me as odd: I had goose bumps. I had a lump in my throat from a commercial. This was a strange phenomenon. Sometimes it takes something very moving to hook the viewer, the consumer, the employee.[7]

From this branding campaign, Liberty Mutual has created "The Responsibility Project" as an exploration of what it means as a company, and as a person, to do the right thing. To learn more about this project, I looked into their advertising firm, Hill Holliday. In building your employment brand, it is a great practice to check out your competition's brand, or brands that you think are quite good. By exploration, you may find your external vendor. Hill Holliday supports a blog on its web site about the Liberty Mutual project. Ernie Schenck, one of the Hill Holiday staff, stated:

It's not every day you get a chance to build a brand message around a core human value like personal responsibility. But if ever there was a company that could do it, *and do it authentically*, it's Liberty Mutual. If you saw the season finale of the hit NBC game show "Deal Or No Deal" last night, you might have caught the opening salvo in our new campaign for Liberty. The 60-second spot is kind of a pay-it-forward concept that demonstrates the infectious nature of doing the right thing and introduces the company's new theme line, "Responsibility. What's Your Policy?"

From the beginning, we've loved the concept of responsibility. As we discovered in research, this is one very hot subject in America. It's such an emotional thing for people. They've got some very strong opinions about it. What it is and what it isn't. As a brand strategy, the timing couldn't be better for Liberty Mutual to embrace responsibility as its brand mantra.

From *attract* to *retain* to *repel*, the Liberty Mutual brand was working the way it's supposed to. And did you notice in Ernie Schenck's opening to the blog, he used the word "authentic"? There it is again, and I'm seeing it more and more. To me, it's a clear indication that authentic may very well be the next HR buzzword — and for good reason.

The comments posted on the Hill Holliday blog highlighted the connection between employment branding and corporate culture. As I read the blog posts, I began to arrange them in my thoughts by Attract, Retain, and Repel. Below are actual comments from the "Responsibility. What's Your Policy?" blog. As you read these, keep in mind that this wasn't supposed to be an employment branding campaign, but it sure serves that purpose!

I was already in the interview process for a position with Liberty Mutual's HR Department when I first read about the ad campaign. After seeing the ad, I sat astonished, tears literally welling up in my eyes as I thought to myself, "If that's how this company chooses to spend nearly $40 million, then THAT'S the company I want to work for." I have my final round of interviews tomorrow. Nothing would make me prouder than to work for a company that invests in society the way Liberty Mutual has done through this campaign. Thank you again for your vision and art!

There were additional postings that provide insight into how this campaign helped retain Liberty Mutual's employees:

> Wow, I've been an employee at Liberty Mutual for eight years, and have always felt proud about the company that I work for, but now, I am incredibly impressed. Our CEO made mention of the new campaign and I've been waiting for it to roll out. For anyone out there that doubts we are the company behind that commercial, we are and the people that lead the company are ... Steve said it best, never have we spent this much money on an ad campaign and I agree whole heartedly that it is the best message we could have. It has to be one of the most moving commercials I've seen in a long time.

As moving as the commercial was for many, some people saw it and were repelled by it:

> Beautiful spot. Too bad we have to get our best messages about being kind to each other from an insurance company that confuses "personal respon-sibility" with social responsibility or human responsibility. The term "personal responsibility" is a buzzword most closely aligned with the Republican mantra for dismantling the fabric upon which civilization is based. Hope it sells lots of policies!

EVP as Differentiator in Job Choice

When it comes to differentiating yourself from the competition, hundreds of HR professionals I have spoken with agree that most companies offer much of the same thing (e.g., same pay scale and benefits, etc.).

I have done some work with call centers and I've found a recurring phenom-enon I've named the Call Center Hop. It doesn't matter if the employees are working the inbound call center or the outbound call center, the skill set tends to be the same. When one call center raises the hourly rate by 15 cents, the message gets out, and employees hop to the call center across the road. Then the other call center notices the exodus of employees and raises their hourly rate by 25 cents (now just 10 cents more), and employees hop back across the road again. This dueling hourly rate can be costly for each organization, so the point is to create a work experience that is worth more than 25 cents an hour to the employees.

But, if everyone offers the same thing, what is going to define a better job? The EVP! Standard "features" companies typically offer health benefits, salary (or some form of compensation), perks (e.g., profit sharing, 401(k), retirement plans), and training and education. This list alone is not going to be enough to differentiate you from your competition, which is why you need to take these features and turn them into emotional benefits — turn them into an articulated EVP. The story would then go something like this …

Compensation: We offer a competitive salary, stock options, performance-based bonuses, and promotional opportunities so that you can grow with us and create the career experience you've always wanted!

Career Development: More opportunities to learn and grow so that you can grow your career with us and get the most important things in your life — things that are not just about your career but your growth and development as a person first, employee second.

EVP Messaging

Once the EVP is developed, your employment branding team can create message maps to deliver the information. A message map would look something like this:

- *Key message/elevator speech.* If you have 30 seconds to tell your main message points, what would you say?
- *Supporting messages.* Describe key messages in more detail.
- *Proof points.* If someone said "prove it," how would you back up the supporting message?
- *Anecdotes and illustrations.* Create an emotional connection by bringing our message to life with stories.

As a reminder, the purpose of creating the EVP is to have a foundation or context on which to build the message, the articulation of the employee experience — the employment brand — to better attract and retain the right employees and repel the ones that just won't fit. By doing so, we are making the assumption that we will have better employee fit, which will increase the ROI of our recruitment and retention efforts. We will do a better job of retaining the employees that fit and repel the ones who wouldn't fit from applying in the first place. So who are these employees, this talent that we're creating the EVP for? Do we create the EVP to attract the best of the best? Or how about attracting just the "average" employee?

Case in Point: The Fallacy of the "Average Person"

I read this article about the average professional football player:

The average NFL player weighs 245 pounds and is 6'1½"
tall. *NFL players are pretty big guys, so nothing shocking
here.* But what's fascinating is that there is not one single
player on the Buffalo Bills who either weighs 245 pounds or
is 6'1½" tall. And, of course, there are no players who match
both averages (i.e. weighs 245 pounds and is 6'1½" tall).

One day we assigned one of our researchers to scour the ros-
ters of every NFL team looking for the average player (weighs
245 pounds and is 6'1½" tall). It was pretty tedious work, so
we let him stop after 10 teams, but he was unable to find even
one player that matched the NFL average.

What's the point of this exercise? Averages lie. Averages are mislead-
ing. Nobody is "average," and if you go looking for the "average"
person, you will probably never find them. Have you ever seen a family
with 2.5 kids?[8]

You see, no one is average. We all bring a unique perspective and experience to
our work every day. As employers, it may be futile to go out looking for the best of
the best, because, like the average NFL player, you'll probably never find them. The
better goal is to attract and retain the right fit, because the right cultural fit will allow
the employee to thrive in the environment they feel comfortable in. Staying authentic and congruent in your branding efforts will support the right fit and placement.
Congruence again comes back to the organizational mission, vision, and values. The
real question is not "Do you have them?", but, rather, can everyone in your company
recite them without looking on the back of their badge, the web site, or a plaque on
the conference room wall? In my recent workshops on employment branding, I ask
the question, "How many of your organizations have a Vision, Mission, or set of
Values?" There are always over 80 percent of the hands raised. Out of those 80 percent, more than 60 percent (about half of the group) say this information is posted
on their web site. But, when I ask for volunteers who would like to get up and recite
those values or mission or vision for the group, I hardly ever get a taker. When I do
find someone who would like to give it a go, we hear from either the owner of a
company (the one who established these in the first place) or someone who gives us
the company tag line and feels that is the mission or vision of the organization. I've
had some people from major corporations be able to do this, as well as a few from
health care systems, and even one from a county government employee. When I've

asked these people how they knew this, they all responded that their organizations had spent "a lot of time" on the development of, the definition of, and, ultimately, the communication of these core values. They all agreed that there had also been accountability built into their performance appraisal systems to ensure employees both understood and could translate these values into everyday work practices.

The bottom line is that it's not enough to have them (your company's vision, mission, or values) posted somewhere, or turned into a designer accessory for your employees to wear around. They need to be transferred in a way that employees can and will embody them. They have to live in the heart — not in the head — of your workforce. It is often easier to speak from our heart about values because they are something that matters; you can attach a feeling to the words.

If you or your employees can't recite your values, then you need to start there, because if your employment brand is built on them, then the articulation of brand will be easier.

A Strong Values Message

McMurry is a marketing communications company that has done an outstanding job of translating values not just into a succinct message but into the cornerstone of their organization. Their web site states:

> Where better to begin the discussion of establishing a relationship than with that which will most guide, impact and nurture that relationship?
>
> At McMurry, our values are guideposts for decision-making and the cornerstones of our culture. A culture that since our beginning in 1984 has encouraged openness, candor and trust. Between management and staff. Between company and client. At a level seldom experienced in corporate America.
>
> Today, the values that first created such a culture are now used to protect and sustain it. Ask those who work here, and they'll tell you that trust has replaced rules. Cooperation has displaced competition. And fairness has removed politics.
>
> Ask our clients, and they'll tell you that their needs precede ours. Egos have no room. And the only agenda is shared success.
>
> There are eight values in all. Each always in play. We hire by them. We manage by them. We treat all in agreement to them. As you're about to see, remarkable things happen because of them.[9]

McMurry goes on to express their values, but, again, they define what each of those values mean to the organization. They have already stated you would be held accountable to these values, and, as the employer, pledge to hold themselves accountable against them too.

Their mission and values are listed along the side of the page, and you can click on each one to get a description and expectation:

- Do the Right Thing
- Help One Another
- Deliver Raving Service
- Produce Quality Always
- Exceed Expectations
- Embrace Change
- Accept Social Responsibility
- Earn a Reasonable Profit

Let's look at the description of just one of these values:

- Do the Right Thing
  - » No value has served us as well or more often.
  - » Do the Right Thing serves as the genesis of trust, the foundation for fairness and the linchpin for empowerment. This value is in fact our operational compass. Because as you do the right thing, the right things happen.
  - » Doing the right thing had us mentor a staff member who made a six-figure mistake into one of the finest managers in the company. It had us create a profit-sharing plan that has distributed millions of dollars equally among staff, regardless of an individual's seniority or position.

Every decision, from the critical to the seemingly inconsequential, is weighed against this value, as it always leads us to doing the virtuous and good.

McMurry says who they are and what's expected. You're either attracted to work there or you're repelled. Maybe you love the idea of "do the right thing" or maybe their anecdote of driving through the night makes you want to move on to the next marketing firm.

For any company to build a congruent and authentic employment brand, values must be true and experienced. As I've said earlier, if an employee takes a job based on what you have told them the culture and experience will be like, and when they get there it's not what you told them, then in a few months they'll be looking for another position.

Con-way on Brand

I interviewed Tom Nightingale, vice president of communications and chief marketing officer with Con-way, a leader in the transportation and logistics industry with more than 30,000 employees worldwide (see Appendix B). We talked about their recent employment branding campaign and how obtaining senior-level buy-in was paramount to gaining support and resources for an employment branding effort:

> **LP:** Why did Con-way undergo an employment branding activity?
>
> **Tom:** We are evaluating our employment brand and codifying our employment value proposition because it is tantamount to our survival in an otherwise commoditized B2B service. We don't produce a manufactured good that our employees can hide behind. If our employees understand and live our employment brand from the first day they are hired until they retire, our customers will see it, feel it, and reward us for it. Once you know your employment brand and what your employees represent in the marketplace, you can attract employment prospects who are consistent with that brand and since they are onboard, more likely to stay with the company because they are a natural extension of your brand.
>
> **LP:** Was the effort considered a strategic initiative?
>
> **Tom:** Yes. It made it to the list of deliverables for me and for our VP of HR.
>
> **LP:** Who owned the branding activity? Was this a combined approach with Marketing and Human Resources?
>
> **Tom:** In a B2B service company, your brand is truly owned by your employees. So, while marketing does the packaging of the employment brand, HR and all constituencies have input and provide guidance.
>
> **LP:** Did you form an internal branding team or use an outside vendor for any part of the initiative?
>
> **Tom:** We used outside firms to help with surveys and both inside and outside resources for design and copywriting.
>
> **LP:** How did you determine budget?

Tom: Certain elements, such as surveying require budget. However, most do not and they just become a gradual evolution and upgrading of existing marketing materials.

LP: How are you measuring the ROI of your efforts?

Tom: We are still in the early stages and our metrics are not universally air-tight, however we look closely at turnover, cost–to-hire, and time-to-hire.

Branding Teams

As the interview with Tom Nightingale states, branding activities are often a mix of internal and external resources.

Results from our 2008 Employment Branding Study[10] of more than 230 companies showed that more than 70 percent of the respondents planned to use or were forming their own employment branding teams vs. going out to external vendors to create their brand. This is a big shift for many organizations, both large and small, that are now under intense financial pressure on spending with external consulting firms. Internal talent has the knowledge and bench strength to do this in many organizations, but there are times when a fresh pair of eyes and external vendors (who have this skill as a core competency) can build a better brand. External consulting firms that have been doing this for years have a deep understanding of employment branding and have extensive experience with what does and doesn't work. Yet, I also caution organizations to be careful of the "repackaged" brands that tend to be sold by some of these creative firms.

I had this experience (discovering a company that repackaged brands for companies) when exploring an alliance opportunity with a large recruitment-advertising firm that conducts a lot of its work in the health care space. We were having our discovery dialogue in a large conference room. Their ad campaigns were framed around the room. Then the thought crossed my mind — how authentic and congruent were these brands they're creating? What diagnostic process were they using to understand the true culture? Where was the quantitative proof that what they had created was the "real deal?" They didn't need any proof, they contended, because they had done enough work with these organizations over the years that they really knew who the organization was and what they stood for. They told me that they had run some focus groups in the past. It was with this prior knowledge they could create a campaign that would be a real representation for the client.

I stood up, grabbed some paper and tape, and began to cover up the name of the hospital or health system that appeared at the bottom of each ad. Then I read the copy.

- We are an organization that is focused on our community and our commitment to caring.
- We value our community so excellent patient care is our number one priority.
- Our staff is committed to caring, which is the cornerstone of our values.
- Our system depends on the men and women who show commitment and caring to our community every day.

Then I asked my potential partner, "So who are they?"

Who are they? They couldn't tell me. They could not tell the difference between the ad for the community hospital, the children's hospital, the cancer clinic, or the city's largest radiology center because they were generic, reused, reprocessed, and re-gifted ads that they charged a boat load for.

They couldn't show me any quantitative research, metric, or measurement that they had used to determine the true employee experience — the authentic brand that they claimed to know. It was a disservice to the hospital and to prospective employees who wanted an authentic work experience.

CHAPTER 4

Values Create Cultures

Why talk about values? Well, if you want to truly understand your organization's culture, you must first start with your values. Values determine the definition of good and bad. Values are at the heart of culture. They form the culture. They are the lifeline of an organization.

Values state what is important to you as an individual and to your organization. In other words, values are what you stand for. They reflect who you are, which in turn affects what you do and how you do it, which is your culture. When you think about values, take a moment to reflect on your behavior and the types of decisions you have made. Do you always act in accordance with the basic beliefs that you hold? Has there ever been a situation in which you had to compromise your values in order to do what you were asked to do by someone else? How did this make you feel?

For most of us, when our behavior is in conflict with our values, we experience stress, frustration, and, sometimes, pain. This ultimately affects what we do, and it affects our organizations.

Like anyone looking to get from point A to point B, businesses need road maps and proper directions. If they don't have clear direction, the best attitude in the world isn't going to rectify the situation. In most businesses, there are two types of maps: maps of the way things really *are*, our reality, and maps of the way things *should be*, our values. We interpret everything we experience through these mental maps. When there is a disconnect or an incongruence, we struggle to reconcile the difference. This is a major challenge for you as a leader. There should be a clear set of directions for reaching your organizational goals and destination. When there is a need for any of your values to change, then let your people know. Otherwise, they will definitely be headed down the wrong street. Our values map must be our reality map.

Why should we be concerned about these incongruencies? Culture can actually become a liability when the core organizational values are not embraced and practiced by everyone in the organization. This breakdown can interfere with your organization's ability to reach its strategic goals, and this can cost you money. **31**

What does this have to do with employment branding? Everything. If organizations know what they are and what they are not, they will be able to attract and retain the right employees and repel the ones that just don't fit. That's how organizational culture and employment branding increase the ROI of recruitment and retention programs (not to mention the profitability of the business). Culture is the driver of behavior in every organization. One of the ways an organizational culture is established or grown is based on the foundation of the organization's values. These values allow us to understand what is acceptable and unacceptable to our co-workers, our customers, and our community. So when culture is clearly defined, it makes it easier for leaders and employees to demonstrate better judgment. Because culture is born out of our values, then we should know how to behave, interact, treat each other, and respond to events and changes in our work environment. This is pretty straightforward, if, from a cultural perspective, we know who we are and who we are not.

Strong leadership teams demonstrate congruence in their actions and behaviors as it relates to their culture (remember the visionary, cult-like cultures from *Built to Last?*). This provides clarity for the workforce and contributes to high energy levels and stronger employee commitment. If that is the case, stronger employee commitment leads to higher retention and increased productivity. This has a trickle-down effect as well because increased ROI equals increased profit. So leaders in high-performing cultures practice what they preach — they *respond* rather than *react*. Employees want to be on the winning team, they want to work for responders — not reactors. Much like in the situation of an acquisition, brands can be decimated by leadership behavior. Your brand is your culture, and any tarnish on your company armor will reflect into your brand.

Companies Increase Consumer and Employee Confidence When They *Respond*

The following examples are from companies that have been open and honest and let their core values drive their decisions in times of crisis.

In 1982 and again in 1986, Tylenol was altered by currently unknown individuals who placed lethal amounts of cyanide in the capsule form of the pain reliever.[1] The result, in 1982, was the death of seven people. The product was voluntarily recalled and Johnson & Johnson, McNeil Consumer Healthcare took a $100 million charge against earnings. The leadership responded to the situation and the organization received much praise for its quick and honest handling of the crisis. The company reintroduced Tylenol in pioneering tamper-evident packaging, eventually regaining its leading share of the analgesic market and changed consumer perception of safe packaging forever. You cannot pick up a consumable product without it having tamper-resistant packing. While this sometimes may annoy us, we always make sure "the seal wasn't broken." Think about the last time you stopped at a convenience store to pick up a bottled water. Did you check the seal? Sure you did! We have become conditioned to check it to ensure our safety.

September 11, 2001. There are hundreds of stories of how companies responded and reacted on that fateful day, but Southwest Airlines' response was immediate. Within one hour after the tragedy, Southwest issued a press release that they were implementing a 100 percent refund policy, period. No questions asked. All you had to do was request it and you were given your money back. It was easy for Southwest to *respond*. They lived true to their values, their culture, and their core.

As reported by NBC News in September 2009, Carat, Europe's largest media network, accidentally sent out an e-mail meant for a few, but seen by many.[2]

> The details of that memo created a wave of embarrassing, negative press. In one fatal stroke of a key, Carat's chief "people officer," exposed staff to a private e-mail sent to her by senior vice president who confirmed what had been rumored, layoffs were imminent. Of course, none of Carat's 14,000 worldwide employees were aware of the decision.

> The problem lies not with the business case for the layoffs, or the mistake e-mail, but rather with the way it was handled. Crisis drives companies to respond or react, whatever way they choose to go, sends a message. In this example, the mistake e-mail demonstrated, by "spinning the bad message" to the employees a position that could erode the trust levels of employees and clients.

> Careful attention was given to word choice, for example. The company was not "downsizing" but rather "right-sizing." "We will be communicating to your team today. Your manager will be contacting clients. We ask that you do not contact your clients to discuss this situation."

> But more delicate care and consideration was aimed at the "critical talent" employees who would keep their jobs. "Let them know we are building for the future," it read. "The actions we had to take, although unfortunate, were necessary to right-size the company and bring in the skill sets we need to effectively service our business and future client needs."

> As for how the news would be spun to clients, many of whom would lose their Carat contacts, they offered this messaging, "Mary Smith will be moving off your business. Now that we understand your business better, we are

replacing her with someone whom we feel will be a better partner for you."
They spun the words to reflect a positive approach to client satisfaction, as
opposed to admitting their own financial setbacks.

We can agree that obviously what happened was a mistake, a human error —
one that many people have experienced. The company did respond immediately to
the organization in the form of an apology, and it is stated that management felt bad
that people found out about the layoffs in this way.

Some companies, if faced with a similar situation, would take more drastic
measures. But this was not the case. They chose to stick by the employee who made
a mistake — a very costly mistake that could tarnish employee confidence and trust
levels throughout the organization, as well as customer confidence or, ultimately,
revenues and profits.

Companies Decrease Consumer and Employee Confidence When They *React*

The leadership at Enron and HealthSouth has been extensively reported on, as
have many others who have been found guilty of wrongdoing in corporate scan-
dals. Leaders in these companies clearly have demonstrated incongruence between
their behavior, their company's culture, and their organizational values. They
behaved in a way that was incongruent with what the company stated its values or
behaviors were. Once that happened, and information began to surface and leak
out, they had to react.

In 2000, Bridgestone/Firestone announced the recall of 6.5 million tires after
the National Highway Traffic Safety Administration issued an advisory that included
information on 174 related deaths. How could the company not know their tires
were flawed in some way? Did quality control completely fail at all of their plants? It
turns out that it did. Most of the tires in question were manufactured at the plant in
Decatur, which was later closed. Or could we assume that someone, somewhere in
the corporation, knew, or even thought that the company might be at fault?

One could assume that they *reacted* to the potential for a massive recall by
trying to divert attention or place blame on anyone other than themselves. Why
was there so much mudslinging and blame associated with this case? It turns out
that most of the incidents occurred on Ford Explorers. Explorers were known to
be prone to rollovers and Ford recommended a lower tire pressure than Firestone
did. There was just enough blame on Ford's part that Firestone could fight them
in court instead of *responding* appropriately to the situation. According to Bridge-
stone/Firestone's stated values, "we strive for the highest quality in our products

and services." If they could have just gone back to that value, admitted that they didn't reach it, and taken appropriate action, they would have come through the crisis a lot better off. In the end, a 2004 class action lawsuit was settled for $149 million against the company. What's worse than that? Their tarnished reputation. I am one consumer that, no matter how good their new company image and brand may be, will not purchase their products.

Another high-profile case going back and forth in the public arena is Merck & Co. Vioxx was introduced and put on the market in 1999. The question here is whether the leadership at Merck was aware of the potential "issues" with the drug. In 2004, a government study was released that shed some light on the inside information that appeared to show that Merck was aware of the issues. Then, in 2005, a physician whistle blower came forward to confirm it. The hit Merck took in the stock price made it evident that many shareholders had lost faith in the organization. Today, many court cases are still pending.

Case in Point: JetBlue Blues

During the week of Valentine's Day in February 2007, a terrible ice storm was predicted to hit the eastern United States. Most airlines preemptively canceled flights, sending passengers home and intending to resume their normal schedules within a day or two. But JetBlue, the eight-year-old, low-fare favorite, thought the weather would break. They believed that they would be able to fly, keeping its revenue flowing and its customers happy. Unfortunately, Mother Nature had other plans and the entire east coast was locked in ice. Passengers were stranded at airports for days. The other airlines were able to get back to normal schedules in a couple days as planned, but JetBlue was in complete disarray. They had employees scattered across the country – planes with no pilots and pilots with no planes. It took them almost an entire week to resume flights.

It might not have been a good response, but what if the leadership at JetBlue went to their core values, their value of providing outstanding customer service, and said, "Let's not inconvenience all of our customers by cancelling flights too early. Let's ride out the storm and get our folks home." I wasn't in the board room or on the conference calls, but what if that was the scenario? JetBlue stuck to their values

and it turned out to be a bad choice, as the CEO said in a full page
Wall Street Journal apology he made the following day.

Another example of a company *reacting* to the situation vs. *responding* to their
values was told to me by a colleague when she was the director of Human Resources
at an international medical-device company. Being ethical, like so many companies,
was at the core of what this successful company stood for, and the belief of the
employees on all levels was that the company should show fairness and integrity in
its dealings with employees, customers, and the overall marketplace. When product
failures became an everyday event for this company, employees wanted to publicly
admit to the problem and fix it, but the leadership had an attitude that it was no big
deal. By this time, consumer safety had become a real concern and adverse effects of
the products were all too common stories in the media.

The first thing that happened was that the organizational leaders allowed
their emotions to get the best of them. One distortion grew into another and yet
another and yet another, until many of those in a leadership role believed that
they were right and the FDA and everybody else was wrong. The truth of the
matter was that they were not living up to one of their core organizational values.
Integrity had blown out the window along with market share. Arrogance (not an
articulated value) was actually stronger than integrity and drove their actions.
This division, which was once the front-runner in this market and had held 100
percent of the market, was now facing criminal charges and had reached the
bottom of the heap. Yes, right down to nothing — zero percent market share —
when they were finally forced to take the product off the shelves. Obviously, this
was a major financial and shareholder value loss, but there was also an exodus of
"A players." None of them wanted to be associated with what was happening at
the company.

Market share plummeted not only because the product was taken off the market, but also because during the span of the next couple years, the company lost
most of its critical intellectual capital. People no longer wanted to be affiliated with
the company. Where did they go? To the competition, of course, and some actually
became the new competition. It took this organization years to regain its credibility
with employees and the marketplace.

In the aftermath, the current leaders of this business brought in high-paid consultants to help focus on values and develop a new code of conduct. They wanted to
ensure it would be on the forefront of everybody's minds and drive every business
decision that was made. The timing decision was poor. Many employees lost their
jobs. All but a handful of the top team members lost their jobs, and some even faced
criminal charges and were subsequently imprisoned.

The take-away here is that it could have been avoided. If the leaders had allowed their core organizational values to drive their business decisions, they would have made the right decision and pulled the product off the market before they were ordered to do so by the government. If they were aware of what values were actually driving their actions, maybe they would have acted differently.

Conducting a cultural assessment can assist you in identifying what values actually drive your actions, and which ones are important to the people, which can prevent such a situation from happening in your organization.

If these managers had listened to their hearts (people were dying as a result of product failures) instead of their heads (which feared the financial repercussions of the truth getting out), they would have seen the need to admit the product failures and work to end them. Instead they acted irrationally. They *reacted* when they should have *responded*. Since values are so important, you must not only embrace them but, more importantly, you must act on them. They must be articulated to all employees, and your expectation must be that all employees will integrate these values into their day-to-day work.

I'm not saying that there is one value or set of values that works for every organization. What I'm saying is that values you profess, whatever they may be, must be more than words — they must be demonstrated.

Trends in Authenticity

JWT, the fourth-largest advertising agency in the world, conducts an annual trend watch. One of the 2009 trends they've identified says that "authenticity will become paramount for brands as they look to regain credibility and trust in the wake of the financial crisis that has seen established institutions topple overnight and many others teeter on the brink. Consumers have lost a great deal of faith in brands once deemed unquestionably reliable, and they are searching for truth and clamoring for transparency."[3] This can also be articulated for employment brands. Potential employees are looking for the same transparency. They go on to talk about how great brands are driven by the consumer experience. They advise one way to exude this authenticity is to involve the customer in the experience of the brand, allowing them to understand the brand in a way that is organic, not contrived. Again, we can say the same here for the employment brand. This is why, in order to create an authentic and congruent brand, you must first identify what that true organizational culture is — and the way to do that is to involve the employees in the diagnostic process.

Organizational Values Exercise

Research collected over a decade, and data culled from hundreds of organizations about their vision, mission, and values, demonstrate that there are two dozen standardized values (see Table 4.1).

Table 4.1. Cultural Descriptors – Values

■ Accountable	■ Ethical
■ Balanced – work/life balance is honored	■ Fair
■ Clear direction	■ Fun
■ Clear expectations	■ Honest
■ Community-minded	■ Innovative
■ Consistent	■ Respectful
■ Continuous learning	■ Results-oriented
■ Customer service excellence	■ Risk taking is encouraged
■ Differences are honored and respected	■ Shared decision-making
■ Effective use of Social Networking	■ Social Responsibility
■ Employee involvement	■ Strong leadership
■ Energized	■ Teamwork
■ Engaged	■ Trusting

One of the most common values is trust. Organizations state that they have to instill trust — trust with their customers, trust with their shareholders, trust with their employees, and trust among co-workers.

Case in Point: The Problem with Perception

Next time you're in a group setting, ask everyone to close their eyes. Ask them to think about a turkey sandwich. Give them half a minute to form the image in their mind's eye. Now ask them to open their eyes and take the next few minutes writing as complete a description as they can about their turkey sandwich. Ask for volunteers to read their descriptions. No doubt you'll find a wide variety of turkey sandwiches. From the simple white bread, turkey, mayonnaise, and lettuce to the more elaborate honey roasted turkey (dark meat only) on multigrain roll with avocado, sprouts, sundried tomatoes, and grape seed oil. Someone might even mention the open-faced, hot turkey sandwich

with stuffing and cranberries. These are just three examples of a turkey sandwich. Ask 100 people, and you'll probably get 100 different
sandwich descriptions.

Simple exercise, sure. But now think about that as it relates to your
company's values – for instance, the idea of trust. Each one of us
has our own definition of trust. In building an employment brand, it is
essential to be definitive. Define all of the values into behavioral terms
so everyone in the organization knows what's expected of them.

Companies may have trust as a definitive value, but have they defined it in
behavioral terms? The answer is almost always "no." Defining values is just as important as having them. Without a definition of the value, you cannot set a metric;
without metrics there is no way to measure accountability for living the value. There
are certain steps you can take to ensure the values you have created are not just
words on a page. I cannot define these values for you. There are too many possibilities of what they mean to each organization, just as there are too many definitions
of a turkey sandwich. The fine point is to define them so they have meaning to your
organization and so they can be demonstrated. Here are some of the steps in the
values congruence process:

- Create a set of organizational values.
- Define values in behavioral terms.
- Communicate values or provide training on the values to all employees.
- Fold value demonstration into performance appraisal system.
- Measure and score employee on value demonstration.
- Reward employee for value demonstration.

Gap Analysis: Values Congruence

Referring back to Table 4.1, place a ($\checkmark$) next to all the values that are important
to *you*. Segment your selection into three buckets — the "must haves" (your top 5
values), the "should haves" (the next 5), and the "nice to haves" (those remaining
values). Now place an "X" next to the values that are closely linked to your organization's *stated* values. Any gaps between what you selected and what your company selected? How do your value priorities mesh with your company's values?
This exercise is one that should be used as you set out to create your employment
brand. Values congruence is pivotal in brand creation, but, even more importantly,
in understanding what your employees really value.

In the Cultural Health Indicator™ we conduct a gap analysis of personal values and company values by asking two questions using the values from Table 4.1.

The first step for employees is: check off all the words you currently experience in our organization. The second step: check off all the words you would like to experience in our organization. In side-by-side comparison, you can immediately see the gaps in what employees would like to have as values (desired state) and what they actually do experience (current state). Armed with this information, you can better align your employment brand to reflect the reality of the work experience so it does not reflect just words on a value statement. Now, keep in mind this assumes that your employees know and understand what their own value system and beliefs are. That is not true for everyone. There is no real way to "make" someone have values, so you have to have a bit of wiggle room and understanding if individuals do not know the answer to the questions.

CHAPTER 5

Attract, Retain, Repel to Increase the ROI of Recruitment and Retention

So far we have created the understanding that organizations need to know what they are and what they are not (from a cultural perspective) so they can attract and retain the right employees, and repel the ones that just won't fit. We'll look at each of these three principles in depth so you gain a deeper appreciation of their importance and the role they play in increasing the ROI of your recruitment and retention programs.

Attract

Attracting candidates can be easy, but attracting the ones that fit your culture is not an easy task. Different industries have their unique challenges and opportunities with recruitment. I was conducting a full-day workshop on how to build an employment brand last year and I asked all the participants to give me their number-one recruitment challenge so that we could brainstorm possible solutions. I was feeling pretty confident about the "expert" advice I was giving … until we got to *Dave*. *Dave* (if that is indeed his name — no last name was given on my registration information) was with Human Resources for the CIA. What was his number-one challenge? He was in charge of recruiting spies. They had to be natural-born citizens of the United States. They had to be fluent in another language and also be able to fit into the national culture of the country they were going to spy on. And, to make matters worse, no one could know they were a spy and they had to pass the excruciatingly extensive background check and reach the highest security clearance. I thanked Dave for sharing his challenges and wished him well. So, rest assured. Unless you're like Dave and with the CIA, there are probably easier solutions to your recruitment challenges.

Let's talk about new strategies that companies are deploying to attract candidates. New technologies have changed the recruiting world for good (social networking is covered at length in Chapter 10). We all know the days of the classified ads will soon be gone. They are not dead yet, but you can track the changes in the publishing world to follow the latest trends of folding newspapers. How many twenty-something's do you know who get their news from reading the paper?

"Attract" techniques are getting more sophisticated, authentic, and clever. Though, it bears commenting on an authentic job posting from the days of old:

> Men wanted for hazardous journey. Small wages, bitter cold, long months of complete darkness, constant danger, safe return doubtful. Honor and recognition in case of success.[1]

You may recognize this as the famous help-wanted ad posted by Shackleton in London newspapers before one of his expeditions to the South Pole. I came across this again recently when a friend of mine sent it out in a piece he was using to attract new employees to the expansion of Onrec.com North America, a new division of Tarsus.

His online ad started with Shackleton's and finished with:

> We are not looking for a traditional come to the office and put in a day types; we are looking for people who have a passion for what they do and who get excited about applying their talents in unchartered waters. It is a frugal start up, but we can promise the coffee will have caffeine even it's not from Starbucks (yet).
>
> We can provide an opportunity to get involved with something that has all the right ingredients to become the fastest growing (and best) employer in the area.
>
> P.S. Unlike Shackleton's ad, both men and women are welcome for this journey — we are looking for talent and passion here, period.

This, followed by contact information, was moving — it had a message, a meaning, and a significant call to action. This was an authentic and congruent description of the way an employee was going to experience the culture and work they were signing up for. This is the essence of *attract:* Tell them what they can expect, but, more importantly, what not to expect.

Here's another example of brilliantly implementing the attract strategy. In 2002, Google ran its first annual programming contest. They had a set of parameters and asked participants to do "something interesting with the data" in whatever way "strikes your fancy." The grand prize was $10,000 and a VIP visit to Google's headquarters in Mountain View, Calif. The outcome was thousands of entries, seven honorable mentions, and one grand-prize winner. What did Google get? Publicity, thousands of free ideas for applications, but, most importantly, they identified brilliance. The ROI of that contest probably came back to them ten-fold just in recruitment alone through practical skills assessment and passive candidates. And that VIP visit to Mountain View? If you had the program winner at your headquarters, wouldn't you discuss possible employment?

Figure 5.1. Employee Satisfaction by Year of Birth

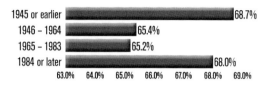

Retain

The retain principle is pretty simple to understand — once you hire an employee that fits into your culture, how do you keep them? Retain is really about employee engagement. Engagement is very connected to cultural fit. It is here that establishing your culture to retain the employees who are engaged, who are connected, who want to be working in your environment, and who fit, can create the competitive business advantage you need.

- A study from Towers Perrin found high-engagement firms experienced an earnings per share growth rate of 28 percent compared to an 11.2 percent decline for low-engagement firms.[2]
- A Manpower survey of call center customers and employees reported that centers with high employee satisfaction also have high customer satisfaction. Alternatively, centers with low employee satisfaction have low customer satisfaction.[3]
- A SHRM report on Molson Coors Corporation estimated that by strengthening the employee engagement the company saved $1,721,760 in a year just from calculating the cost of a potential safety incident. It was calculated that the average cost of such an incident for an engaged employee was $63.00 compared to $392.00 for a disengaged employee.[4]
- A study by Gallup yielded responses from more than 3 million employees. The engagement break down was as follows:[5]
  - » 29 percent of the U.S. workforce is actively engaged, 55 percent is not engaged, and 16 percent is actively disengaged.
  - » That means that 71 percent of the Americans who go to work every day are not engaged in their job.
  - » This equates to businesses operating at one-third of their capacity.

There was an employee engagement follow-up study conducted by Blessing-White in 2008. While their sample size was much smaller than the Gallup study (based on 7,500 responses from global companies), it still has some interesting statistics to use in those "charts and graphs" we need to create for our C-suite executives who still may see this as soft stuff. The key finding in this study was fascinating. They found that North American employees were among the most engaged worldwide. They also did a great job of connecting engagement to retention. They state

> There is a clear correlation with 85 percent of engaged employees indicating that they plan to stay with their employer through 2008. Moreover, engaged employees stay for what they give, they like their work, where disengaged employee stay for what they get (favorable job opportunities or job security).

BlessingWhite also drew a clear line between the engaged employee you want to retain and the success of your business.

> Engaged employees are not just committed. They are not just passionate or proud. They have a line-of-site on their own future and on the organization's mission and goals. They are enthused and in gear, using their talents and discretionary effort to make a difference in their employers quest for sustainable business success.

Ask yourself, "How can I determine if my employees are really engaged or disengaged?" First, measure it with a quantitative metric. But if that is not the path you can go down at the time, simple observation might give you an indication. Some random morning, go into work early, head up to the highest vantage point of your building and watch. Watch the employees getting out of their cars, off the bus, or walking along the path to the entrance. What are they doing? Are they excited? Are they walking with their heads down, sluggish, looking like they obviously feel like they have something better to do than walk into your building? If this is what you observe, then it's probably how the employees are feeling, and they will probably carry that feeling along with them most of the day.

There also is a correlation between employee satisfaction and birth year (see Figure 5.1). The findings in the BlessingWhite study were aligned with the research done by Press Ganey in 2008. Press Ganey is the noted authority on data collection on patient satisfaction indicators for most health care organizations. They are well respected and do an outstanding job of filtering out a lot of information and distilling into logical data we can all understand. They published an interesting graph in their *Employee and Nurse Check-Up Report* that provided responses from more than 202,514 employees at more than 423 facilities nationwide between January 1 and

December 31, 2007. The finding suggests that employees born between 1965 and 1983 report the lowest satisfaction rate of all employees, followed closely by those born between 1946 and 1964. These two groups of employees make up the largest percentage of the overall workforce.

This data gives us an indication of the potential for targeted communication and employment branding programs in our recruitment and retention activities. Press Ganey states:

> … understanding the motivations of employees of different age groups can also help facilities to retain employees. Request employee input and suggestions as employees from each group will provide ample information about what they need from their careers and their employers.

There it is again, that advice to get out there and ask the employees for their ideas, opinions, voices, and stories. By doing this one simple thing, you will discover all the information you need to build an authentic, congruent employment brand that will be compelling and guaranteed to attract, retain, and repel.

There is a movement in Human Resources that is focused on adding a deeper understanding to employee engagement, and that movement is dedicated to measuring presenteeism. The approach is based on trying to measure the loss of productivity (how "checked out" the employees may be) from the employees who are in attendance at work. We have always measured absenteeism. Just look around the office and count the empty chairs at active work stations; you've measured your absenteeism.

What if the person is *in* the chair but they aren't really *there*? They're focused on something other than their work. Maybe they are monitoring an active eBay auction, collecting money for the football pool, talking to their sister on the phone, or updating their online dating profile. This trend of *checking out* while at work is growing, not shrinking, and I have seen it cost organizations plenty in lost productivity.

Some organizations allow employees to take care of personal business on company time. The leaders of these companies know that we all have personal lives. We all have bills to pay, personal calls to make, and parent-teacher conferences to attend, and these things can weigh heavy on the mind if not attended to and taken care of. So the school of thought here is to allow employees time to take care of these personal tasks without feeling like they are sneaking or stealing time from the company. Take the time to take care of yourself and then you will be more focused when working.

According to Paul Hortop, with network security consultant firm, Voco, a quarter of workers' time online is personal.[8] He says CIOs and CFOs have no idea how much time is spent browsing eBay auctions, online dating, or social networking sites. It is virtually impossible to monitor what site each person is on without looking through more data than it would be worth to calculate. Other activities such as downloading music, games, and movies eats up not only the employee's time, but precious bandwidth and can open an organization up to lawsuits for downloading contraband to their site.[9]

Kevin and Jackie Freiberg refer to these disengaged employees as "dead people working." They feel that this is…

> how to refer to those people who are just showing up, yes they arrive on time, they leave on time but they are psychologically, emotionally and intellectually checked out! Work is just a mortgage payment. Work is something that you just need to get through so you can live the rest of your life. We've only got one shot in their world — shouldn't we embrace that opportunity?[10]

Moreover, they state that, "if you want to hire people who love what they do, get cozy with crazy. Push your culture out of its comfort zone with radical people and revolutionary ideas." I have stated that leaders create cultures. They foster them, grow them, and can decimate them all at the same time. So this cozy with crazy idea would have to be embraced by the CEO. I have done a lot of organizational culture work in the past 15 years and I have met a lot of CEOs who would not be very cozy with crazy, but it sure would be a welcome change if they were!

In 1999, when I was doing the research for my earlier book,[11] I interviewed more than 100 CEOs. From their feedback, I developed a "loss of productivity" calculator. The CEOs were asked, "How much time do you think is lost in productivity during times of change and transition?" The answers were astonishing — anywhere from two hours to a whole day was the reaction. The full days accounted for the employees who, due to the changes, experienced a high level of stress, which caused absence and even an increase in the use of EAP dollars.

So we took into account size of organizations, enormity of the change, whether it was a merger, new leadership team, IT transition, etc., and came up with a standard calculator that many tell us is on the conservative side. During times of change and transition (they are too numerous to list), the average employee has up to two hours a day in lost productivity. This is something you can calculate to determine the potential loss in your organization. Here is an example:

> 1,000 employees x average hourly wage of $15/hour = $15,000
> $15,000 x 2 hours/day in lost productivity = $30,000
> $30,000 x 20 days worked in a month $600,000
> $600,000 x 12 months = $7,200,000 in lost productivity

This example is for an organization with one shift running Monday through Friday. If you work in a hospital or a manufacturer that has three shifts, seven days a week, ensure you capture that in your numbers. This can be staggering given the changes and challenges businesses are facing today.

The airline industry is a perfect example of why employee engagement is critical to the success of your business. In this customer-driven industry, the way these employees feel — especially the pilots — has a direct correlation to customer satisfaction, and possibly customer loyalty, which equates to hard dollars. These are the men and women whom we rely on to be engaged with their jobs, focused every minute of every pre- and post-flight, and committed to the company they work for. Here are two different messages from the pilots' associations to their CEOs that speak directly to employee engagement.

On September 4, 2007, United Airlines pilots paid for a full-page ad in the *USA Today* with their perception of United's leadership demonstrated behaviors.[12] This sends a message about their level of engagement, but, more specifically, their level of employee satisfaction. The piece was titled UAL Management's Labor Day Message to United Pilots: "We're Not Interested."

> This Labor Day, as our country honored and celebrated the contributions of the working women and men of America, United Airlines continued to turn a deaf ear toward its most valuable assets: its pilots and our fellow employees. Since our airline exited bankruptcy 18 months ago, United's senior managers have enriched themselves through stock options and, in some cases, pay raises. These windfalls were made possible by the sacrifices and sweat of labor.

It's interesting that much of what is covered in the full-page dialogue can be confirmed in other media sources and articles. The ad continued,

> the level of management compensation is a clear indication that United senior executives are intent on building a kingdom of wealth for themselves while ignoring the struggles of their employees who continue to live with bankruptcy-induced wages and working conditions.

This kind of a message does not come from employees who trust their leadership to do the right thing or who are happy with how the company is being run.

They went on with five more focused bullet points, all ending with the United management's response of "we're not interested." While this ad was paid for by the "dedicated pilots of United Airlines," the final call to action spoke volumes to me about the level of unrest and dissatisfaction from one of the most important assets of this organization. "Mr. Tilton, it's time you started listening to our needs for a change. United Airlines is not about you. It's about all of us." And as I finished reading the article, I sure hoped that the *us* includes the consumers who choose to fly this airline.

It bears repeating, this is a tough industry. There are lots of pressures for the pilots and the leadership of these businesses. I'm not sure if pilots' associations get special rates for full-page ads from *USA Today*, but another full-page ad appeared on May 21, 2008, this time from the Southwest Airlines Pilots' Association.[13] This ad, however, was markedly different. It was a goodbye message to Herb Kelleher. This again got me thinking about employee engagement, trust in leadership, and employee satisfaction. It was a great picture of Herb in a cockpit with a pilot in his seat. Herb, of course, has his signature "crazy" grin going on. The ad says,

> THANK YOU HERB! From cocktail napkin to cockpit, Herb Kelleher paved the way for the most spirited Company in airline history. As you step down from the SWA Board of Directors, the pilots of Southwest Airlines would like to thank you, Herb, for 38 years of positively outrageous service to our Company and our pilots. It has been an honor and a privilege.

So after hearing about these full-page ads, I would like you to think about which airline you would feel the most comfortable flying with given the state of the pilots' association's comments. And, after that, think about which airline you might choose to work for, given the picture the pilots have painted for us. The answer seems pretty simple.

Repel

HR professionals understand the need to attract and retain talent. It makes sense. But what about the need to repel? In my opinion, it is as important, if not *more* important, than the other two. You need to repel the candidates who just won't fit into your culture to increase the ROI of recruitment and retention.

We know that cultural fit is important in getting the right employee to apply. We know it is up to the organization to take the potential candidate through a real experience during every touch point in the interview process so they can peek behind the curtain. They glean information about the company from what they can find on the web site, social networks, blogs, press releases, and current and former employees. So how do companies boldly state what they are and what they are not in order to weed out a bad fit from applying in the first place?

I think the best and certainly the most brazen example of this, no matter what beliefs or convictions you hold, is the U.S. military policy commonly referred to as

"Don't Ask, Don't Tell." This political hot-button issue has gotten a lot of press since the early days of the Clinton administration, but it has been mandated by federal law. The military leadership is clear about the "type" of person that they don't want.

OK, so how do you repel candidates without the benefit of it being mandated by federal law? Lots of companies are doing it and with a lot less political heat.

A discussion of the repel principle wouldn't be complete without talking about religion. Companies with religious ties tend to hire from within their own religion. I once had an HR director attend my full-day intensive workshop on building an employment brand not once, but twice. During our lunch break the second year, I nudged her and jokingly said that since this was her second time attending, she should really just hire me to do some employment branding work for her organization. "Oh, we don't need to build an employment brand," she claimed. I looked at her dumbfounded and asked the obvious question, "Then why did you pay to attend my workshop two years in a row?!" She told me that she needed the credits for her SPHR certification and that my session was great the first time she attended, so she wanted to come a second time. However, she worked for a Baptist university and they did not conduct any recruitment outside the Baptist community, nor did they hire "outside" vendors. This rule of thumb was also confirmed by another faith-based university. Now this isn't something they necessarily advertise, but it's pretty well understood that those who get hired outside the religion are few and far between.

There are corporations with religious affiliations that can either attract or repel potential candidates, depending on their religious persuasion. Let's look at Chick-fil-A. This privately-held corporation is the second largest chicken-based fast-food chain in the United States and brings in billions of dollars annually. There are company-owned and franchised restaurants in malls, airports, as well as freestanding Chick-fil-As. All Chick-fil-A locations are closed on Sundays. They are the only major fast-food chain to do this. Why do they do it? Founder S. Truett Cathy, a devout Southern Baptist, said, "Our decision to close on Sunday was our way of honoring God and directing our attention to things more important than our business. If it took seven days to make a living with a restaurant, then we needed to be in some other line of work. Through the years, I have never wavered from that position."[14] According to their web site, their corporate purpose is "to glorify God by being a faithful steward of all that is entrusted to us and to have a positive influence on all who come in contact with Chick-fil-A."[15] These are definitive statements — Chick-fil-A is rooted in religion. They are clear on what they are and what they are not.

Am I saying that Chick-fil-A only hires Southern Baptists? With more than 1,400 locations, that certainly is not the case. What I am saying is that Chick-fil-A is clear on what they are. As a potential candidate, you know this going in. You may love the idea that, regardless of your shift or position, you will have every Sunday off, guaranteed. You might be completely repelled by the corporate purpose and fear that you'll try and be recruited into a religion that isn't your own. So again, just like U.S. military, whether you like it or not, you know what they are and you know what to expect by joining the organization.

During my presentations, I ask attendees to raise their hands if they want to be a "Nordie." I never get any takers. Then when I ask who wants to work for a company known for having the best customer service on the planet and hands shoot in the air. It's interesting that just by calling their employees "Nordies," Nordstrom has repelled so many potential candidates right off the bat. But not so fast … candidates who can get past the silly moniker are very proud to be "Nordies." Legend has it that a harried executive, on her way to the biggest meeting of her life, spilled coffee all over her suit while getting into her cab. With literally just minutes to spare, she runs into Nordstrom and grabs the first "Nordie" she sees. He takes one look at her and says, "Walk with me, walk with me, walk with me." As they zip up the aisle, he tells her to look at the mannequins. "Size 14 top and 10 bottom, am I right?" She nods and points to the suit she likes. He grabs the correct sizes off the rack, sends her to the dressing room to change while he races off to the cash register with her Nordstrom card in hand. In the three minutes it takes her to change, he's already rung up her purchases and she's able to run out the door to her cab, waiting at the curb. Once she's gone, he realizes that she's forgotten her wool coat. He's able to pull up her home address through her Nordstrom account and it's shipped back and waiting for her before she even gets home from her business trip. Amazing customer service, right? Oh, I forgot to mention that he had it dry cleaned first. So now do you want to be a "Nordie?" Nordstrom is another organization that is very clear on what they are and what they are not.

The best example of an organization that knows the value and potential ROI of *repel* is a story about the Southwest Airlines interview process, back in the late 1980s. It is said that a call for pilots went out and thousands of resumes came in. When the process was narrowed down, groups of 30 were called in to interview and were put in a large conference room. An HR representative bounces into the room, welcomes the prospective pilots, and tells them how special they are to be there. She holds up a blue short sleeved shirt and shorts and tells them before they get started with the interview process, they had to head into the locker room to change into the maintenance uniforms. Once they're changed, they'll meet her on the other side to continue the interview process. One potential pilot raises his hand and says, "Excuse me, but I have black knee high socks on under my trousers, and if I put on those shorts I am going to look like an idiot." She replies, "No you won't — this is Southwest! Now everyone come on!" and out of the room she goes. Next thing you know, all the candidates get up and start heading to locker room, but this fellow holds back, shakes his head and says, "Forget it!" and walks out the front door. In that very moment, he self selected out and Southwest brilliantly repelled a potential employee that did not fit their culture.

Am I saying that he was a bad pilot? Of course not. In fact, he might have been one of the top pilots in the room but *he wasn't the best for Southwest*. He didn't fit. He wouldn't be the pilot who comes on the intercom after landing at the gate and says, "All rise!" He is probably a great fit at Continental or Delta but not for Southwest. Southwest Airlines' hiring philosophy was and still is "hire for attitude." Libby Sartain, the former vice president of People at Southwest Airlines said, "If we hire people who don't have the right attitude, disposition, and behavioral characteristics to fit into our culture, we will start to change that culture. The recruiter's primary role is to make sure it's a good cultural fit."[16]

When you (as an organization) know *what you are* and *what you are not*, and can clearly articulate that to all potential candidates, you support your ability to repel the candidates that just won't fit. This is where the real hard-dollar savings are experienced.

CHAPTER 6

The Mad Hatter:
Human Resources as a Marketer

Why does Human Resources need to put on the marketing hat? Easy: Marketers see the value chain from start to finish. Think about sales flyers and coupons you receive in the mail or that free download via the Internet. They will most often have an event or incentive code that you need to enter in order to receive your free gift or discount. This is the tracking system marketing professionals use to identify the exposure, measure acceptance, and quantitatively track the ROI of the marketing campaign. We have established several things about Human Resources' role in the development of the employment brand:

1. Ensure you have senior-level support for understanding your organizational culture and creating an authentic and congruent employment brand.

2. Assess or survey the employee population using a validated quantitative and qualitative diagnostic to determine what your true organizational culture is and is not. If you do not have the resources to gather this data, start with the last set of data collected from the employee satisfaction or employee engagement survey, as this may provide insight into the current culture and employee perception. If you do not have any data to start with, you will need to collect it, somehow. Whatever way you choose to collect this data, I suggest you do a quick cost-benefit analysis of external vendor vs. internal resources before you commit to a data-collection activity.

You can collect data in a variety of ways:

- *Survey vendor.* An external vendor can collect third-party neutral data via phone survey, Internet, or paper and pencil.
- *Create your our own survey.* Develop it yourself and deploy it on any of the free survey platforms offered on the Internet.
- *Focus groups.* Gather groups of people and ask them the same set of questions while capturing their answers on flip charts. If you have a technology center or training room at your disposal, there are companies that provide group data-collection technology that can be collected from desktop stations. Keep in mind, focus groups take up much more time and resources than Internet-based surveys.

3. Review your organization's vision and mission. Determine if these *live* in your employees' experience. Examine the organizational values. What are they? Have they been defined in behavioral terms? Have they been included or folded into the employee performance evaluation process? Are your rewards and recognition programs built to support or enhance the values?

4. Determine your plan of action to develop your EVP. Who will need to be included? What pieces do you already have developed that can be enhanced?

5. Determine if you will need a formal employment branding team. Will this team be an advisory group or a working team that will pull all the pieces together to create a brand?

Case in Point: Creating a Culture and Brand Assessment Tool

Traditional employee opinion surveys do not get at the real business issues. To know if your workforce is satisfied or dissatisfied is not enough. You must ask yourself the question, "Why are my employees satisfied or dissatisfied? Why are my indicators high or low?" Measuring the satisfaction levels of benefits is not enough, and to measure morale is foolhardy; morale is not a thing, it cannot be measured. Why morale is high or low is an outcome of how a business is structured and how it operates – this is your culture.

When constructing the assessment tool, certain things that must be considered. Surveys should:

■ Be developed in such a way that the right things are being collected and measured.

■ Provide clarity for leadership as well as for the entire workforce.

■ Focus on the governing principles, formal organizational procedures and systems, informal practices, environmental factors, organizational characteristics, and organizational values that frame the direction and actions of your organization.

■ Serve as a baseline marker for the "current state" of the organization.

■ Go below the surface and understand the behaviors occurring that are helping or hindering your organization's ability to achieve its business/financial goals.

■ Determine how employees understand the vision, mission, and organizational values.

- Contain statements that suggest balance, alignment, consistency, and peace. Terms such as "trust," "clear," "understood by all," "protect," "reliable," and "clear communication" should be used to speak to the "calm" within an organization.
- Be connected. All sections of the survey must be connected, and no compartmentalization should occur. This allows you to take a holistic look at the connections.
- Capture stories, histories, assumptions, customs, rituals, and language. These factors play an important part in employee satisfaction.
- Identify status of structure, planning, technology, and people valuation by the organization.
- Identify the subcultural issues of conflict, communication, decision-making, and how the organization applies these issues of decisions to the formal procedures.
- Examine disorganization, flexibility, resolved and unresolved conflicts, and self-regulation and self-direction, which are essential to the creation of a healthy work environment and a healthy performance of the work.
- Define the ability of the organization to identify the gaps and connectivity that exist in their performance and thinking.
- Have a goal of creating satisfaction parameters.
- Place heavy emphasis on the change process.
- Focus on the trust and empowerment factors for employees.
- Seek to find best practices within the organization to celebrate and duplicate.
- Include a thematic component. Themes are perspectives of critical values, processes, and beliefs about the organization that often are present, but not fully conscious by all who work within the organization. This portion of the survey will serve to validate the findings of the quantitative section of the survey. This should include elements such as: trust, collaboration, creativity, diversity, innovation, and bureaucracy.

Before we dive into the employment branding process or determine the need to form a branding team to create that authentic and congruent brand, we need to better understand why (and how) HR professionals need to think like marketing professionals.

Thinking like a marketer means tracking, measuring, and evaluating ROI constantly. Candidates may see our logo, our brand, our ads, but they may not be *motivated* to really look at us. There is nothing driving them to open their eyes to the possibilities with a company they pass by, potentially every day.

ROI is becoming increasingly important in the HR world. Unfortunately, the approaches have been unsophisticated and largely irrelevant to the needs of top executives and shareholders. One of the fundamental flaws with measuring ROI for Human Resources, or even Organizational Development, is the expectation that we show a "positive return" on our projects. While this approach may be easy to do in other areas of our companies, ROI of the human system is not as easy to reveal on a financial statement. There are fundamental tools like cost-benefit analysis that can be deployed on some HR projects, and, these days, most HR professionals are using good metrics when it comes to hiring employees and it will become increasingly important to do so. Charts and graphs are what attract attention, but keep in mind that, many times, metrics have hidden costs that aren't always taken into account:

- Cost-per-Hire (CpH). What is the actual cost per employee you hire?
  - » This can be difficult to benchmark between industries, regions, demographics.
  - » Most CpH calculations do not take into consideration the opportunity costs or risks associated with not filling the position. If the position goes unfilled, what tasks have to be assigned to other employees? What tasks may have to go undone and what opportunities might not get achieved by allowing these to be incomplete.
  - » Example: Annual costs = $1,000,000 (at budget)
  - » Number of hires = 5,000
  - » CpH = 1,000,000/5,000 = $2,000 annually
- Cycle time or TTF (time-to-fill) is calculated from the date of the requisition to the date of hire or start date. This is hard to calculate because it is dependent on your culture and hiring practices. The typical cycle has standard steps:
  - » Requisition is generated by the hiring manager
  - » Human Resources develop internal posting
  - » Human Resources develop external posting
  - » Position posted
  - » Candidate process time
  - » Interview and candidate selection
  - » Drug test, background check, and pre-employment screening
  - » Candidate offer extended
  - » Wait time on candidate accept/deny
  - » Offer accepted
  - » Start date determined and open requisition closed

- Average annual salary of new hires
- Recruiter work load (number of requisitions they have per week, month, quarter, year)
- Screening ratio — interviews to hire (resume process time and background checks)
- Acceptance rate — how many candidates accept the position offered vs. deny

Perhaps these costs sound like they belong more in the realm of the CFO than a marketer or HR professional, but the exploration and discussion must take place in your organization so you can determine exactly how you're going to calculate the ROI of recruitment and retention. We're going to look at what could equate to some heavy expenses associated with the creation of an employment brand. If you don't begin the process with a well-thought-out tracking mechanism and financial target, you could potentially miss capturing the ROI or hitting your financial targets all together.

Another metric to keep in mind is the one that links behavioral change and valuation. According to E. Ted Prince, "conceptually this approach is very attractive. But to be able to work and to be measured requires an underlying model that links the behaviors change resulting from HR programs to be linked formally with financial performance and valuation outcomes."[1] This sounds like a daunting shift in the way we view Human Resources, but one that may become the norm (or at least it should) in the near future. Prince also agrees with the school of thought that, "one of the best ways to measure this impact of valuation is through surveys of executives and managers who have undergone the program to improve their financial impact. Do not reject using traditional project based ROI measure, providing they are used appropriately and in the circumstances. Project based ROI measure can be used as an important component in the valuation approach." To reiterate, you must measure progress with a quantitative metric that you can track over time. They can be as complex as the valuation approach or as simple as tracking information on a spread sheet.

Jac Fitz-enz is a well-respected expert in this area and provides formulas for tracking recruitment and retention efforts. His perspective is that as companies are becoming aware of the effects simple measurement can have on the bottom line the more inclined they are to focus on their human capital.

Back to thinking like a marketer. Are you checking to figure out which job boards send you the most candidates? From those candidates, are you tracking how many are interviewed and then hired? From those that are hired, how long do they stay? Sheer numbers alone are not enough to go on.

If Monster.com sends you the most candidates, but they are the least likely to get hired, should you continue to post on Monster? If CareerBuilder.com sends you the most candidates who get hired but have the shortest tenure, are they the best job board to spend your recruitment dollars on? Remember that not all points are equal, so you should incorporate weighted performance. You need to determine priorities of relevance and importance, specific to your recruiting needs. You have to measure quantity and quality.

In the initial interview or screening process, are you asking candidates how they found out about the position? Most of you probably are, but what are you doing with the information? This should prompt you to create a database from these answers. Remember the old saying, "you have got to measure what you treasure"!

Measurement will help you track the ROI of your advertising dollars as well as set a metric for your employee referral programs. Employee referral programs may be the most cost-effective way to recruit candidates. In the Gallup Q12 question about having a best friend at work? This may sound simple, but it's important to your employees! In the Gallup Q12 the amount of employees that belong to social networks? This can be a very valuable tool to support these employees to recruit for you. It is suggested that the average MySpace page is visited 30 times a day. This translates into nearly 11,000 hits a year — hits on a page that costs you essentially nothing. Go to MySpace and type in your company name. You might be surprised to see what pops up. This is a ripe venue to show off your EVP... for free. Think about that ROI.

Review your employee referral program. It may illuminate data that shows that a low percentage of candidates are coming from employee referrals. If you find that a low percentage of candidates are being referred by current employees, it might be a data point that raises important questions and compel action to:

- Re-evaluate (or maybe even create one if you don't have this in place) the value of your employee referral program.
- Benchmark your employee referral program with other organizations.
- Interview employees to determine why they are not referring people.

Maybe the only reason employees aren't referring candidates is because they're either not asked to or there is no incentive for them to do so. Many organizations today are using employee referral programs. When I was in health care, we offered $3,000 to employees who referred an RN, and the nurse stayed for one year. Employees received $1,500 at the time of hire and $1,500 at the end of the year. Even if you left the organization, you still got the referral fee. If you are in an industry that has a lot of entry-level positions, offer incentives to employees to get people to apply. Give something away that's affordable or unique to your organization — something that an employee or potential candidate would see as value and will motivate them into action.

Some companies are creating marketing gimmicks to get potential customers and employees to take a second look at them. Jobing.com pays for their employees' gas if they wrap their car or truck in the company's marketing material! This unique employee benefit program began back in 2001, when Jobing.com was a staff of only 10 people. The idea came from CEO and Founder Aaron Matos, who wanted to find a cost-effective, unique way to create awareness for the company within the community. Not only would a Jobing.com mobile do that, but it also created a cool way for employees to earn some extra money. As of 2008, there are nearly 300 Jobing.com employees across the country, and 61 percent of them drive a wrapped vehicle, including the CEO.

In late 2008, corporate America was consumed with the reduction of operating costs, while maintaining or increasing profit. Mike Nale, a managing partner of The Brand Management Group, asked in a June 2008 ERE blog,

> What if that's not enough? What if the goal you have in mind right now is really going to hurt you in the long run? Would you be willing to take a risk? Increase while everyone else is decreasing? That is precisely what I am telling you to do. Growth during a recession in order to promote your brand is important, and talent is the key to growth.
>
> "It is well-documented that brands that increase advertising during a recession, when competitors are cutting back, can improve market share and return on investment at lower cost than during good times." — John Quelch, a professor at Harvard Business School.
>
> This is true with respect to recruiting. Branding your company as the best place to work during a recession is critical to the process. Trust me, top talent is looking, especially now.
>
> When you start to grab these players during a recession, it will positively impact productivity, so whether you are a search consultant advising clients, or an HR executive, you need to think about this scenario as a way to impact your business positively over the long term.[2]

The simple fact is that many recruiting and HR operating budgets don't include money for branding anything. Regardless of whether they paid to create it, every organization has a brand. It's their earned reputation for how they treat employees. This brand is not built through clever ads on job-posting sites, nor through multi-channel branding campaigns, or any other promotional method. A corporate brand is shaped by three primary things:

1.   How a company actually treats its employees
2.   What those employees say to other people about how they are being treated

3. What the company's former workers say about how they were treated while
    they were employees

A number of larger employers (for example, Google, Microsoft, Oracle, and
Kellogg's) can have employer brands that are shaped by national media coverage,
but this is a rarified breed. For most companies, employer brands are simply earned
reputations. Those reputations usually exist narrowly in industry niches, occupation-
al specialties, or in multiple slices of demographic clusters that are either geographi-
cally or occupationally close to the company.

You cannot expect to hire or recruit based on industry, geography, or knowledge, skills, and abilities (KSAs) alone. The most beneficial thing is to hire for
cultural fit. Now you have an understanding that people don't just "take jobs" any
more but that they are after the experience. Create a brand that sells the experience.
Only then will you have a greater ROI for your efforts.

If the goal of attracting and retaining quality talent is what you are after, then
there are a few things that you can do to ensure your brand strategy becomes a
distinct competitive advantage. Partner with your marketing department. The
relationship can prove to be beneficial — and not just when it comes to following
marketing guidelines or not "messing with the company logo." There are critical
elements to marketing that must be paid attention to, such as research, data integrity, consistency, satisfaction, and feedback. Marketers understand that customers
have numerous choices, and that is why a successful marketing campaign delivers a
"brand experience."

There are great arguments for deploying both an internal employment branding team and contracting with an external vendor for brand creation. These can be
done separately or in tandem. Again, keeping consistent is going to be a key factor
in congruence. I have a friend in the recruitment advertising world who is often
asked, "Why should we hire an external vendor to develop our brand?" She always
fires back with a question for them. "Would you cut your own hair?"

The Conference Board conducted a study, years ago, on engaging employees
through employer brands. The results — albeit too old to use in today's world —
were interesting. There was a great sidebar story about a case study at IBM. The
marketing staff at IBM had done considerable work on the corporate or product
brand, and the company wanted 100 percent alignment between the product brand
and the employer brand. Obviously, it was essential that both were clearly aligned
with IBM strategy. To ensure that goal, the team developing the employer brand at
IBM used the same methods, the same consultants, and even some of the same internal team members who had worked on the corporate brand. Tom Marchan, vice
president of Employee Relations, stated that they had intense cooperation, especially

from the marketing people. Marketing was extremely interested in the employer brand because the product brand reinforces the employment brand and vice versa.

Marketing creates the "image" of your organization. Creating interesting and lasting impressions is key function, as well as an art form. They are the ones who know how to use viral branding, emotional branding, mind-share branding, and even cultural branding. It is not all graphics and images that work; they deploy a cognitive model of branding. Together, these models account for nearly every consumer-branding initiative today. The most successful and durable brands have been built by the compulsive reiteration of the distinctive benefit supported with rational agreements and emotional appeals.[3] Many of the greatest brands have "brand essence," which is the DNA, genetic code, and brand soul.

If you think the importance of iconic brands are overblown, think again! In 2007, Dr. Thomas Robinson of the Stanford University School of Medicine set out to study the overall influence of a company's brand. Robinson and his colleagues conducted a taste test with 63 preschoolers. The children were offered five pairs of foods and asked if they tasted the same or to point to the one that tasted better. The food, taken from the same order, was wrapped in either McDonald's packaging or unbranded packages in the same color and style. The preschoolers overwhelmingly preferred the taste of burgers and fries when they came in McDonald's wrappers. The preschoolers even preferred the "McCarrots" and "McMilk." Amazing, right? Even the youngest of consumers can discern their favorite. McBranding — preschoolers are lovin' it.[4]

So what does a recognizable consumer brand have to do with employment branding? People make assumptions about your culture and their potential employment experience based on your product and consumer brand. It's much easier for iconic brands to attract and repel candidates than it is for lesser known companies. Think of it like this: You're 16 and looking for your first job. You've grown up eating at McDonald's. You have an almost Pavlovian response to McDonald's: McDonald's Happy Meals have toys, toys make me happy, thus McDonald's makes me happy. What's the first fast-food chain you're going to consider working for? You guessed it — McDonald's.

While product brands are built on these models, employment brands that are built on your EVP can and will do the same. Consider Yahoo! I have done work with them on cultural diagnostic projects. Yahoo!'s EVP was created in the context of their culture so it would communicate the *value* of working at Yahoo!, not just the features. For example, a typical description of a company's compensation package would include features like a competitive salary, stock options, bonus, and promotional opportunities. Yahoo! was able to go a step further to communicate the value of what that meant to the employee — "so that you can grow with us and can create the career experience you want." Another value of working at

Yahoo! was relationships and connections. So while you can work with some of the brightest people around in a dynamic and challenging environment, the value to the employee is "so your work makes a difference." Yahoo! understood how to leverage their iconic brand into their employment brand.

Creating a Branding Team: The Players

In the 2008 employment branding study with Kennedy Information, we found that of those surveyed, 72 percent said that they do not use an external vendor for employment brand creation. You may be like those respondents and choose to create an internal team to develop your employment brand. If you do, here are several things you might want to consider before forming the team:

- Ensure you are getting a good cross representation from the organization. Many times, we pick all the "A" players for team projects. Reach out to some of the biggest cynics in your organization — they will tell it like it is, which is exactly what you want.

- Try to include some of the line employees or folks who service your employees. They are the ones who are "in the trenches."

- By all means, reach out to marketing and PR. In the employment branding study I conducted in 2006 and 2008 (see Appendix A), more than two-thirds of the respondents agreed that employment branding was the responsibility of Human Resources. But this does not mean that marketing and PR should be excluded. They are the people who can support you to ensure that your employment brand, while not exact, can be (and should be) aligned to your consumer brand. Keep in mind that many employees may be attracted to work for you given your consumer brand. Remember the Starbucks, GE, and Liberty Mutual stories? Don't forget to weave this message and meaning into your employment brand. Also keep in mind that this employment brand is going to have to be communicated to your current employees as well. Collaborate with PR or internal communications so the message you create will be easy to transfer both internally and externally.

- Next, bring the recruiters and hiring managers onto the team. Here is where you will get information on how the current talent pool is responding to your current messaging.

- Invite IT or IS. In the creation of an employment brand, it is a given that you will have to make changes to your web site, career site, and, possibly, your intranet. IT will be the ones asked to make those changes, so include them from the start of the process. You may also decide to conduct an internal survey. Again, IT or IS will be asked to support this effort.

IT will be a key player in your employment branding programs, as the Internet and your career site may be the first line of introduction for your efforts. According to Peter Weddle, an e-brand is not...

> an advertising jingle or a stirring statement of the corporate commitment. Perspective employees will not accept these statements at face value anyway; they will do some field testing on their own. They will want to sample the attributes the company claims to include in its employment value proposition by an evaluation how they are treated during the recruitment process.[5]

And in today's world, that process often will begin with the first touch point of an e-brand experience.

Employment Branding Costs

What are the associated costs and savings of using an internal team vs. an external vendor? There are many considerations to take into account when considering both hard-and soft-dollar costs. In our employment branding study, we asked about executive buy-in for branding as well as what metrics companies where using to track the effectiveness and ROI of their branding efforts. There was not a lot of hard data provided back to us. One recurring theme was "metrics, what metrics?" If you use an internal team, make sure you develop a quantitative metric to track your ROI. Another theme in our employment branding study was that leadership didn't want to invest the money in an employment branding effort. One comment summed up much of the responses: "When I told leadership that we should invest $75,000 in an employment branding campaign to *hire better engineers*, they said they would rather spend the $75,000 and hire an engineer." This is why metrics are so important! You must be able to prove to senior leadership that attracting, hiring, and retaining the right employee is better than having any employee and will save you money in the long run.

Many of the costs of an employment branding campaign depends on company size, revenues, senior leadership support, internal bench strength (or the need to bring in an external vendor), and the profitability of the company.

There are two ways to look at the ROI of the creation of an employment brand. One is the cost associated with building the brand in order to attract new talent. The second is to retain the employees we know are a good fit and want to keep in our organization. To this end, Carol Morrison states,

> although logic would suggest that retention initiates take place after the employees have been part of an organization's workforce for a period of time,

> some experts now say that the time to commence retention efforts is during
> the recruitment process — before individuals are hired.[6]

She cites 2006 research from the Institute of Management and Administration that found what appears to be an oxymoron: Retention before the fact is one of the top five strategies that firms are using to address their concerns about finding and keeping the talent they need.

The Employment Policy Foundation stated that replacing an employee, for whatever reason, costs about 25 percent of that employee's total annual compensation. Across industries and compensation levels, the retention cost ranges, on average, from $6,803 to $19,465 per employee (in 2005 dollars).[7]

Portraying an employment brand that is not authentic to the true culture of your organization can also lead to a significant "human loss." Take one executive salary from the past year that you felt was a "bad hire" and take 75 percent of the annual salary and use that for a branding effort. Why 75 percent? The resources it takes in a bad hire or *non-fit* situation can be added up this way:

- Relocation cost
- Sign on bonus
- Stock options
- 401(k) payment
- Training — getting up to speed on the company
- Benefits plans
- Administration costs: new phone lists, intranet updates, web site updates, PR or press releases, new administrative assistant changes

We know that losing valued employees is costly. That is the exact reason for my contention that we need to create a brand that will *repel* the wrong candidates from applying in the first place.

With the changes and popularity of social networks and online tools, purchase influence no longer belongs to a few individuals who can afford large ad campaigns; it belongs to everyone and it's all about influence. How do you motivate people into action, how do you get them to recommend you, and how do you get them to get their friends to recommend you?

Jane Paolucci, senior vice president of Marketing for Popular Media Inc., published a list of the 10 steps to building a consumer brand, and it is relevant to the creation of the employment brand.[8] I agree with the flow and steps she has set out and feel it is a great guide post to use in this process.

- *Know your audience.* Understand their social networking, online activities, and demographic data.

- *Create a compelling experience.* Make sure that experience drives an action in line with your marketing goals.
- *Create a message that sparks conversation.* You want them to distribute your message through their social networks, so make it one they will "click" or opt-into.
- *Frame your story.* Give them something to get started, like a message or content to share and an engaging web site they can invite friends to visit.
- *Measure, track, analyze, and optimize.* Start with a defined strategic goal and choose the right metrics.
- *Constantly seed traffic.* Long-term success will require you to be out there trafficking.
- *Make it easy to connect.* Make it easy for people to share your content with others.
- *Tout your success.* Nothing succeeds like success. Get testimonials.
- *Segment your influencers.* Your program should build an opt-in database of participants so you can track in the future.
- *Keep your influencers engaged.* The most important part of the campaign is the follow-up. Once someone has demonstrated a willingness to act on your behalf, keep them engaged.

I am seeing a shift in organizations where Human Resources, communications, and marketing are merging their resources to create positions that focus specifically on employment branding. They are beginning to pool, share, collaborate, and team up to create real and authentic brands.

We will continue to see a rise in these positions as external vendor dollars dwindle and the importance of branding to increase the ROI of recruitment and retention continues to rise.

Case in Point: Looking for Director of Employment Branding

I recently found this position description for a director of Employment Branding for The Home Depot. The position did not specify what area it would report into, but it is interesting to note the key account-abilities and speaks to the KSAs a dedicated branding position can have.

Here is a highlight of some of the major tasks, responsibilities, and key accountabilities:

- 15 percent create employment brand strategy, budget, and resulting marketing activities.
- 10 percent partner with marketing department and public relations to leverage and execute programs.
- 15 percent consultative role with HR vice presidents and store managers.
- 10 percent recommend solid marketing plans to support internal staffing initiatives.
- 10 percent identify trends, data, and critical factors that influence staffing levels and conduct research as necessary.
- 20 percent provide leadership to the employment marketing team.
- 10 percent analyze marketing needs for various subsidiaries and divisions, track the effectiveness of marketing execution.
- 10 percent oversee outside marketing partners selected to support the employment for media service, marketing support, job boards, etc.

CHAPTER 7

The Great Divide:
Generational Differences and
How to Create an Employment
Brand that Bridges the Gap

Generational differences for cultural fit are wide and diverse. If you want to appeal to a multi-generational workforce, generational differences pose challenges in creating an employment brand. We understand that different generations have different values, so how do we create brands that will attract and retain them?

Before getting into the branding aspect of the generational divide, we are going to do a quick review of the generations that the employees fall into in order to ensure we have the same frame of mind going into this exploration.

A generation refers to a group of people born during a span of a certain number of years and shaped by similar events, trends, and technologies. Back in the 1600s, your life experience would be similar to that of your parents and grandparents. That is certainly not the case now. Most demographers agree that the generations break down in the following manner, with the years varying only slightly from one expert to another.

Baby Boomers (born 1946-1954)

These are the children of "The Greatest Generation" as Tom Brokaw named them, born after World War II. This is the first generation that had widespread access to higher education. Their worldview was shaped by the space race, sexual freedom, social movements (civil rights, women's, environment), and assassinations (President John F. Kennedy and Rev. Martin Luther King Jr.).

Their critical years for joining the workforce — between the mid-1960s and the end of the 1970s — were a period when most countries enjoyed significant progress. This led to great expectations of success. Currently, this group occupies positions of higher corporate responsibility and has the largest proportion of workaholics in history.

People who were born in the 1960s were being told, "We stand today on the verge of a new frontier." But the minimum wage was $1![1] The average American salary was $4,700 a year.[2] And, in those days, all we needed was love, right? That's the mindset that's built in these Baby Boomers, but the work ethic is different. Now that translates into a lot of different things. You take a manager, 45 years old, born in the 1960s, and now they're being asked to manage someone with a different worldview, a different work ethic, or are being managed by someone with a different work ethic or outlook on life.

Our first Baby Boomer retired on January 1, 2008. About that time, it was estimated that 30,000 Boomers will retire each day in the United States, many in the public services or the government sector. By 2012, there will be an unprecedented labor shortage. However, the worldwide economic downturn has changing that calculation. Economic pressures, the weak dollar, and the plummeting stock market have forced that older worker to work longer, to stay in the workforce well into their sixties, and some say they will have to stay into their seventies. The U.S. economy, with so much emphasis toward service- and knowledge-based skills, leaves few jobs that would be wholly inappropriate for the mature worker. Mature workers usually have a good work ethic, pay attention to details, and accomplish tasks, resulting in higher productivity. The shifts in the economy also find many of these Boomers with reduced 401(k)s and minimal retirement plans. And let us not forget that in many organizations we need to keep these older workers, because many of them are the keepers of knowledge — historical knowledge we can not necessarily afford to just toss away and think we can start from ground zero or rely on the new graduate to bring with them. Knowledge management systems (technology for managing and disseminating knowledge in organizations) are being developed in organizations to ensure we don't lose this precious intellectual capital.

In 2007, RetirementJobs.com surveyed more than 400 workers, 50 years and older, and asked what they were looking for at retirement age and "nearly 70% ranked flexibility or lifestyle integration as their top consideration in choosing an ideal retirement job."[3] It was noted that organizations needed to start thinking in this direction to attract this demographic. The bottom line from a cultural perspective is that organizations need to incorporate these alternative arrangements in their quest to retain skilled and quality talent.

The First Consulting Group and the American Hospital Association published the study, *When I'm 64: How Boomers Will Change Health Care.*[4] It outlines the expectation in changes in health care that will need to occur to continue to cover all the Baby Boomers as they retire and reach eldercare age. The report shows how Boomers will leave an indelible mark on the health care system. There will be more people enjoying their later years (see Table 7.1), but they'll be managing more chronic conditions and therefore using more health care services by 2030.

Table 7.1. Boomer Generation and Future Estimation

Year	Boomer Age Range	Estimated Number of Boomers
2000	Ages 36-54	78 million
2010	Ages 46-64	75 million
2020	Ages 56-74	70 million
2030	Ages 66-84	58 million

Many organizations have realized that the great Boomer exodus they feared isn't happening. They are shifting their culture to better align for Boomer fit to attract and retain those mature workers with new programs and incentives. The following are a few award-winning examples of companies that are doing just that.

The AARP named Centers for New Horizons to its list of Best Employers 2007.[5] Sixty-one percent of the Centers for New Horizons employees are 50 years or older with an average tenure of 12 years. They look for senior placement agencies to target mature workers and retirees. They tout that their workplace culture is one of continued opportunities. Full- and part-time employees working at least 20 hours a week are offered in-house classroom training, online training, certification classes, and the chance to take temporary assignments in other departments through team projects. They also have great health care coverage, prescription drug coverage, vision care, and dental insurance. The extra mile here is that they offer a plan to assist with out-of-pocket health care costs that might not be covered under their current plan. They also see the option for alternative work arrangements, flextime, and telecommuting where possible.

The retailer CVS/pharmacy won the 2007 Large Business and Aging Award from the American Society on Aging[6] for recruiting, training, and retaining mature workers. CVS/pharmacy believes mature workers are cost-effective because of their loyalty, worth ethic, and how they relate to older customers. The CVS mature workforce programs include:

- Snowbird/seasonal placements (for those workers who spend their winters in warmer areas of the country and return home in the spring), and easy transfers
- Senior Pharmacist Legacy Mentoring, pairing mature workers with young technicians
- Flexible benefits for part-time workers
- Partnerships of excellence where CVS collaborates with government and public organizations to recruit their mature workers

L. L. Bean was named to AARP's 2006 Best Employers for Workers Over 50 list.[7] Their strategies to attract and retain mature workers include:

■ Retirees back-to-school program, where they were eligible for tuition reimbursement

■ The "swap book," where they can pick, trade, or give away shifts to another employee

■ Attendance bank, which provides time to be used without disciplinary action for time needed away from work for sickness, accident, or personal reasons

■ Long-service celebrations

■ On-site exercise programs

■ Fifty percent discounts in the company cafeterias and special "retiree hours" for the employee store

Many companies are employing more creative means to keep their mature workers, but it definitely takes a shift in culture, behavior, and attitude in order for organizations to be successful. You do not just "flip the switch" to a culture of inclusion of mature workers or develop these programs overnight. They all take a well-thought-out plan and resources to back them up. But companies understand that it is much more economical to keep their intellectual capital and the resources they have invested than to try and replace them with someone who is not already inculturated into their organizations. It's like the sales motto that selling to an existing customer is much less expensive than selling to a new customer.

In *Workforce Crisis*, the authors give us a great list of honorable mentions:[8]

■ Wal-Mart has an outreach program where they recruit and provide job fairs at senior centers. These cost less than the slick job fairs they have to run on college campuses.

■ Days Inn compiles a job bank that is shared across the company and helps to recruit seasonal employees. Knowledge sharing between the franchises and corporate properties reduce duplication of effort and cost.

■ Mitre rehires experienced temporary and part-time help, mostly engineers, through "Reserves on the Ready" on-call program during times of peak need. The flexibility of this arrangement, and the ability to receive pay and retirement benefits, allows valuable mature workers a form of phased retirement.

■ Monsanto has found that 10 percent of their workforce comes from the "resource re-entry center," which allows employees to re-enter the company as a part-time employee. This has reduced agency fees (ROI) and helped with knowledge loss.

■ Dow Chemical provides a form of flexible retirement where the mature worker can down shift into less demanding roles, such as coaching or teaching.

- Intel partners mature workers with younger workers on a six to nine month assignment to transfer knowledge. The pairs go to class together and set up a contract stating the goals of the partnership. This is much like the formal mentoring programs at CSX and Southwest Airlines.

Generation Jones (born 1954-1965)

You might not be too familiar with this generation by name because they have generally been lumped in with the Boomers. However, with the election of Barack Obama, born in 1961, this historically overlooked generation has gained new prominence. Members of Generation Jones were young children during the Summer of Love for the Hippies and missed participating in the protests for civil rights and Vietnam. They did, however, experience Watergate, the Cold War, and the Cuban Missile Crisis. Jonathan Pontell named this generation, and their name carries a double meaning. This generation is so populous that the competition of "Keeping up with the Joneses" ensued. The "Joneses" were the fictional people who lived next door and had all the latest consumer goods; they caused envy and inspired consumerism and greed. This generation also popularized the slang term, *jonesing*, meaning "to crave." According to Pontell, this generation, as children in the optimistic 1960s, had huge expectations, and then were confronted with a different reality as they came of age in the pessimistic 1970s, leaving them with an unrequited, jonesing quality.

Generation X (born 1965-1979)

Coined by Douglas Coupland in 1991, this generation was shaped by the end of the Cold War, the fall of the Berlin Wall, and the first Gulf War. They were the first "latchkey kids," which basically means they let themselves into the house after school since both their parents were part of the workforce. They were told to "Just Say No!" They were also shaped by the Reagan presidency, the AIDS epidemic, the recession of the early 1990s, and the advent of mass media.

This generation has the best academic training and international experience in history. They have begun to make a break with traditional patterns of behavior, demanding a more informal environment, and abandoning hierarchical authority in favor of a more horizontal and flexible structure. They have pioneered policies that involve flexibility and conciliation. This generation is rich in entrepreneurs because personal initiative predominates within a context of skepticism toward large enterprises.

Generation Y (born 1980-1997)

This is the last generation born wholly in the twentieth century. They experienced their "coming of age" during the millennium, so they are known as the "Millennials." Their childhood was shaped by the technology boom: Internet, cell phones, TVs in every room, DVDs, iPods, YouTube, and Facebook. They are the first generation completely comfortable with technology.

In the 1990s, there was a total shift. The digital age really began and the minimum wage went to $5.15. There were 23-year-old vice presidents of Human Resources, and the dot-com companies either produced billionaires or went bankrupt. People were paying hand-over-fist for Internet-savvy web designers. Hundreds of blue chip, *Fortune* 1,000 companies moved manufacturing and back-office operations offshore. The feeling that "the company doesn't care about me" became even more prevalent. Generation Y is the first in history to have lived their entire lives with information technology. It is not easy for them to understand the world without it. They are *technology-natives* and all the rest of us are *technology-immigrants*. I bet you can think of some people in your organization who don't even have their technology visas!

Like members of Generation X, their childhood was comfortable and prosperous. They are more individualistic than earlier generations and demand autonomy in their opinions and behavior. Generation Y is entering the workforce saying, "Hey, look at me. I'm going to *work to live*," vs. your old mindset of *live to work*. They emphasize personal activities above social and labor considerations.

Generation Y sees the organization differently, they communicate differently, and their work ethic and work lifestyle is extremely different, but do they really *think* differently? Research done by the Pew Research Center Publications[9] reveals that the typical 21-year-old (who was in kindergarten when the World Wide Web was launched) has logged 5,000 hours of video games, sent or received 250,000 e-mails, instant messages, and phone text messages, talked 10,000 hours on a cell phone, and spent 3,500 hours online.

Generation Y is comfortable communicating with a lot of different people through technology. This type of interaction has become the norm for Generation Y. It's Generation Y that is really leading the charge in bringing diverse thinking into organizations, even more so than the HR profession.

Sharon Birkman Fink says that they are just now entering the workplace in force and there are potentially 80 million or more of them. For Millennials, everything is about speed, customization, and interactivity; the more digital the better. They love freedom and responsibility, and have been given both throughout their lives. As the products of "helicopter parents" and similarly inclined teachers who have hovered over them and provided praise, stimulation, and support, Millennials expect consistent and positive feedback, and relish change. They bond closely with their peers (as much through technology as through personal interaction), and have a strong focus on following the lead of the latest changes by their physical and online friends.[10]

We live in a multi-cultural world. The day is approaching when it will be difficult for people to choose just one ethnic category on demographic surveys. Generation Y appears to be more open minded about diversity. While racism still exists, Generation Y didn't grow up with the obvious disparity and rampant racism that previous generations experienced.

Think of this in the context of organizational cultural fit. In the past, people have sought to work with individuals who are like them. That preference will dwindle in the coming years. Diversity will be the way for companies to fuel growth by tapping into multi-cultural markets, and much of this is composed by the new Generation Y population.

Years ago, we were hyper sensitive to affinity groups. We talked about having an inclusive culture, and the way to do that was to offer opportunities for like-minded individuals to get together and share ideas, feel comfortable with difference, and have the platform to discuss anything in an open environment. We offered brown-bag lunches, blocked off conference rooms for open dialogue groups, and created the affinity corner in the company's monthly newsletter. But how inclusive is this?

Today's social networking has replaced these old affinity groups, and Generation Y and social networking go hand in hand. (The benefits and pitfalls of social networking will be covered in detail in the Employment Branding Tool Kit in Appendix A.)

If your organization does not embrace these social networks, in the context of cultural fit, then you may be irrelevant to a segment of the population. I can already hear the groans, "Why can't employees just go to work so we don't have to accommodate special interests in order to get good candidates?" Because if you don't, then another company will and they will likely seem more appealing to employees you desire to recruit and retain. And trust me, if you just stick any old generic brand on your employment brand, employees will know the difference.

One of the trends spotted in the JWT Trend Spotting report from 2007 was "truthiness" in branding. JWT stated that, "Truthiness, the American Dialect Society's 2005 Word of the Year, coined by comedian Stephen Colbert, is defined as the quality of stating concepts or facts one wishes to be true, rather than concepts or facts known to be true."[11] Pretty logos and slick packaging will become far less persuasive as consumers do more research and look harder for the facts. Watch for truthiness in branding to fall out of style while truth in advertising re-emerges." Organizations can threaten their own future if they do not adapt to the style and differences that Generation Y brings. If the organization will not adapt or shift, they are probably not going to be attractive to the younger employee. And if that happens to your organization, be ready to miss out on some serious energy, creativity, and innovation they will bring to another organization, which just might be your competition.

Generation Z (born 1998-present)

This generation has yet to be officially named, but some other names are Generation V (for virtual) and Gen @. Their childhood is being shaped by the September 11, 2001, attacks in the United States (and although this was directed at the United States, it had global implications) and the War on Terror. Depending on the length and severity of the current recession, it may also affect this generation's worldview. With the election of the first African-American president and the expansion of gay rights, this generation may have an even more open view of diversity than any of the preceding generations.

Generational Challenges in the Workplace

In their 2008 study, Next Step surveyed more than 3,000 companies to research multi-generational workforce challenges.[12] The respondent group represented all four generations, ranging in age from mid-twenties to mid-sixties. They represented a variety of industries, including technology, life sciences, manufacturing, and professional services with revenues from under $1 million to more than $100 million. The study reported the number-one challenge companies are facing with a multi-generational workforce is predominantly due to the difference in communication styles (see Figure 7.1.)

Figure 7.1. Challenges in Working with Different Age Groups

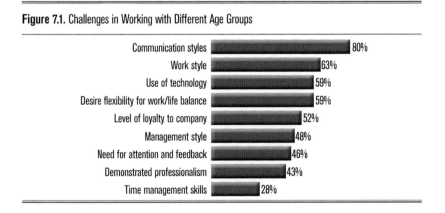

Communication styles	80%
Work style	63%
Use of technology	59%
Desire flexibility for work/life balance	59%
Level of loyalty to company	52%
Management style	48%
Need for attention and feedback	46%
Demonstrated professionalism	43%
Time management skills	28%

Sometimes it appears that Generation Y only knows how to speak and write in acronyms (see Table 7.2). You have to ask yourself, in the context of creating an employment brand, how are you going to attract, retain, and repel multiple generations of employees with this dichotomy of communication styles?

Table 7.2. Alphabet Soup:

Abbreviation	Meaning	Abbreviation	Meaning
OMG	Oh my God!	G2G	Gotta go
LOL	Laugh out loud	WAS	Wait a second
BRB	Be right back	LMK	Let me know
S2S	Sorry to say	MYOB	Mind your own business
L8R	Later	HRU	How are you?
IDC	I don't care	JK	Just kidding
TTYL	Talk to you later	B/C	Because
B	Be	C	See
K	OK	R	Are
U	You	Y	Why

Source: Shally Steckerl Chief CyberSleuth JobMachine, Inc. http://www.jobmachine.net/shally

The other interesting statistic that came out of this study was the information they surfaced about the attributes that applied to Generation Y (see Figure 7.3). They found that Generation Y's most valued attribute was their use of technology.

Figure 7.3. Valued Attributes of Millennials entering the Workplace

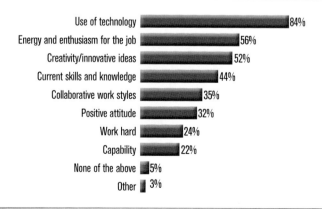

Next Step's overall findings suggest that in order to maximize employee engagement and productivity, companies must consider the different perspectives, needs, and motivators of their workforce, as well as the challenges that come with integrating the various generations.

You have employees with widely differing views about what the organization is going to do for them. Obviously, this will have a profound impact on your EVP, and, ultimately, your employment brand. Your challenge will be creating strategies to retain the Boomers, engage Generation X while staying on the cutting-edge of technology to attract the fickle yet innovative Generation Y.

CHAPTER 8

Sustainability and Branding:
Going Green

We've all heard that green is quickly becoming the new black. Just like organizational culture was touted in the 1990s as essential for business success, social responsibility seems to have taken its place during this decade.

The big question is, "Does social responsibility *really* matter to candidates?" Since green recruiting is such a new idea, there is conflicting information about it. Organizations and independent recruiters must determine whether or not social responsibility is important, not only to Generation Y (many of whom say it is among their top criteria in their job search and that they may even take less pay to work for a green company), but to Boomers, Generation X, and Generation Z.

Regardless of the many points of view and studies that have been conducted, the contention still stands that organizations must be smart and get started on formulating plans, implementing programs, or advertising their green policies. Companies that don't begin to fold green into their recruiting efforts will be left behind by their more savvy competitors.

One component of a company's employment brand is its sustainability practices. This can cover the entire organization or focus specifically on the HR function. Sustainability is not a "flavor of the month" or a new concept. *Fortune* 500 companies have been doing it for years, and your organization might have the right stuff … you just might not be leveraging your green practices and programs in your recruitment efforts.

In 2007, John Sullivan wrote,

> While candidates of all generations have begun evaluating potential employers based on their "greenness" few in recruiting have leveraged this hot topic in recruitment communication and activities.[1]

He goes on to say, "Individual recruiters need to make the firms' environmental stance a critical element of their sales pitch to potential applications and candidates."

In early 2008, at an HR Star Conference in San Francisco, I asked a room of more than 300 HR professionals how many of their companies had an environmental policy. Only 10 percent of the room responded that they did. But, when asked if their company recycles, more than 80 percent responded "yes." If you recycle, you have an environmental policy but you just may not be leveraging the messaging in your branding efforts. Some of the participants didn't see the connectivity between what recycling is to environmental policy. This practice is easy to leverage on their careers' site, on their consumer site, or communicating it to employees. It's all in the positioning of how you communicate your true organizational culture.

Leverage and Communication

Timberland

Our mission is to equip people to make a difference in their world. We do this by creating outstanding products and by trying to make a difference in the communities where we live and work.

Our place in this world is bigger than the things we put in it. So we volunteer in our communities. Making new products goes hand in hand with making things better. That means reducing our carbon footprint and being as environmentally responsible as we can.[2]

Whole Foods

We believe in a virtuous circle entwining the food chain, human beings and Mother Earth: each is reliant upon the others through a beautiful and delicate symbiosis.[3]

Whole People

We recruit the best people we can to become part of our team. We empower them to make their own decisions, creating a respectful workplace where people are treated fairly and are highly motivated to succeed. We look for people who are passionate about food. Our team members are also well-rounded human beings. They play a critical role in helping build the store into a profitable and beneficial part of its community.[4]

Whole Planet

We believe companies, like individuals, must assume their share of responsibility as tenants of Planet Earth. On a global basis we actively support organic farming — the best method for promoting sustainable agriculture and protecting the environment and the farm workers. On a local basis, we are actively involved in our communities by supporting food banks, sponsoring neighborhood events, compensating our team members for community service work, and contributing at least five percent of total net profits to not-for-profit organizations.[5]

Evaluating Mainstream Organizations

While these examples are a good indication of valuing sustainability on the human side of the business, it is kind of intuitive to find given who their core customers are. But what about more mainstream organizations? I looked at Microsoft and discovered nothing special about people and sustainability. I looked at Cisco and could not even find how to connect to their career page from their home page, a process that we will look at in Chapter 10. Finally, in looking at Texas Instruments, I found they have a small link to corporate sustainability and their career section at the bottom of the home page:

> Sustainability, social responsibility, philanthropy — no matter what you call it, Texas Instruments is proud of our long legacy of outstanding corporate citizenship. It is our commitment to accountability for our social, environmental and economic impact around the world. [They repeat the same sentence on their career page.][6]

I was not effected or moved by these statements, and did not feel they do a good job of leveraging sustainability in their messaging.

We expect companies like these, as well as Patagonia, Lands' End, Coleman, Tom's of Maine, and Ben & Jerry's, to be leading the green brigade. They have a market presence and consumer brand that appeals to environmentally-conscious consumers and employees. It comes back to values congruence for the potential employee. We make assumptions that their consumer brand is congruent with their employment brand. What they are saying in their external marketing seems to match their internal marketing and recruitment efforts.

We are just now starting to measure the effectiveness in having a green brand in relation to recruiting efforts and ROI. But we know that there are companies like Honda, Starbucks, Goldman Sachs, Xcel Energy, and GE that are attracting media attention and, in turn, boost recruitment and retention efforts. Medium to small organizations like Bain Consulting and Taxi! Taxi! (a Santa Monica, California-based transportation company whose entire fleet of cabs are hybrids) are advertising their efforts to attract both internal and external customers.

Forbes magazine ran a June 2007 article about Bain Consulting, one of the world's leading global business consulting firms.[7] They say green is the new gray pinstripe at Bain. Two second-year associates had a passion for the environment and it caught the attention of the partners. Their passion turned into a program that launched competition among many of the offices for reducing printing, using water bottles instead of paper cups, and posting signs that encouraged turning off lights in conference rooms when not in use. Did this program have a significant impact on the organization? It sure did! The company has pledged to be carbon neutral by mid-2009, and they have reduced the paper cup usage by 40 to 60 percent for a potential savings of around $8,000 annually. They have also reduced the amount of printer paper they use by 15 percent, thus lowering the amount of printer cartridge replacements by five percent, adding up to another $40,000 or so per year. The green proof is in the hard-dollar savings. This story demonstrates an organization that followed its value of "valuing its employees" and empowering them to follow their passion and interests. It also represents a prudent management that looks to contain costs and reduce waste.

"Living our Values — Starbucks Commitment to Social Responsibility" is a recent brochure that describes its organizational values. The approach is an excellent example of the cultural *fit* factor in action; the ability to appeal to current employees and customers who may be looking for a job and hold sustainability as a personal value. The brochure states:

- 100 percent of our coffee will be responsibly grown, ethically traded
- 100 percent of our cups will be reusable or recyclable
- Will contribute over one million community service hours per year

The first thing you notice about the brochure is that all of the pictures were *real people;* real Starbucks people with real stories. The second was that the message seemed real and authentic. The Starbucks mission statement is prefaced with "We believe the mark of a socially responsible company is one that adheres to its deeply held values. At Starbucks, our values are embedded in our mission statement and guiding principles. We strive to live our values every day."

"Mission: Establish Starbucks as the premier purveyor of the finest coffee in the world while maintaining our uncompromising principles as we grow."

"The following six guiding principles will help us measure the appropriateness of our decisions:"

1. Provide a great work environment and treat each other with respect and dignity.
2. Embrace diversity as an essential component in the way we do business.
3. Apply the highest standards of excellence to purchasing, roasting, and fresh delivery of our coffee.
4. Develop enthusiastically satisfied customers all of the time.
5. Contribute positively to our communities and our environment.
6. Recognize that profitability is essential to our future success.

In 2006, General Electric (GE) teamed up with MTV's 24 hour College Network to offer the "Ecomagination Challenge" to college students. The premise was simple and a great way for GE to capture environmentally friendly exposure, which would also boost their corporate image to potential consumers and new employees. Whatever their motives were, they offered $25,000 in grant money to develop and implement an environmental project on the participant's college campus. More than a hundred proposals were collected. The grand prize went to a team from MIT for a solar-powered processer. The smart move for GE was that, on every electronic page of information for this program, they had a link on the bottom to "Jobs at GE." Even subtlety mentioning a career at GE was a great employment branding opportunity that they knew enough to leverage throughout the contest period.

If you don't believe "going green" is here to stay, think again. Former Vice President Al Gore won an Oscar for *An Inconvenient Truth*, and Live Earth concerts have swept the globe. On March 29, 2008, the global initiative for Earth Hour celebrated its second anniversary. It was lights out for an hour across the world. The idea started in 2001 when 2.2 million Australians and 2,100 businesses in Sydney turned off their lights for an entire hour. This massive collective effort reduced Sydney's energy consumption by 10.2 percent for that hour, which had the equivalent of taking 48,000 cars off the road for one hour.[8]

Waste Management, a national trash removal company, thanks us with a full-page ad in the *USA Today* for helping them to recycle enough material in 2008 to fill the Empire State Building over 11 times.[9] They are working to triple that amount by 2020 and have created a web site to help us help them: www.thinkgreen.com.

Virtually every organization touts being green, but does "going green" mean the same thing to your employment branding efforts as it does for your consumer image? Most agree that it means lessening a company's environmental footprint, but, like our quest to define "organic" years ago, we are stilling working to establish criteria for being "green."

Generation Y and college grads are concerned, and conscious about how their behavior impacts the environment. What they consume, how it's packaged, what they drive, and where they live are conscious choices that are made every day. As you can imagine, who they work for also plays into these decisions. In the context of employment branding, green information should be positioned appropriately on the company web site, career page, and in a recruitment video. This approach can be a significant differentiator or at least the tipping point for a company that's interested in attracting top Generation Y talent that would be a good cultural fit. There is no argument that the interest for sustainable practices is increasing.

- Eighty percent of current employees want to work for a "good company" (one that has a good reputation for environmental responsibility), and this percentage is expected to grow to 90 percent in the next 10 years.[10]

- Seventy-seven percent of recent MBA graduates would forego some income to work for a firm with a credible sustainability strategy.[11]
- Companies, overall, that use sustainable business practices are approximately three percent more profitable than those that don't.[12]

While there is some counterpoint to these studies, my perspective is that going green, even in tough economic times, is a must. Companies that do not give consideration to being green, or just provide "green washing" lip service, may be passed over by potential candidates who don't wish to be associated with that kind of an organization.

While presenting at the HR Round Table for the National Society of Professional Engineers in November 2008, we launched into a dialogue around being a LEED (Leadership in Energy and Environmental Design) green building firm.[13] Some of the HR professionals from the top engineering firms around the country talked about their experiences with new graduates who were applying to their companies for jobs and asking to only be assigned to LEED projects. While this is only one example, it shows that the current generation cares about the environment and wants to align themselves with organizations that share their same value system.

Many people, when judging corporations, weigh social performance as equally as financial performance. We have become consumers with a conscience. We want to keep our environment healthy and have clean air to breathe, but we also want to be financially secure and comfortable. There are many corporations, large and small, that are finding that you can have it both ways. McDonald's has come a long way in environmental awareness, from serving up Big Macs in non-biodegradable, plastic-foam cartons to repackaging its fast-food items in recyclable paper and cardboard.

Sometimes going green can actually create a windfall. Take the case of Ray Anderson, who reinvented his billion-dollar international carpet-manufacturing business, Interface Global, Inc., on the precept that a corporation could comply with the law and still make a profit.

In Anderson's case, the shifts resulted in greater operational efficiencies and cost savings. And as a direct result of the new business philosophy, Interface was invited by The Gap to bid on the job of carpeting their new headquarters because of this environmental consciousness — and won. Anderson's crusade is one example among many proving a new rule in business: *Profits and social responsibility are becoming inseparable.*

Interface Global, Inc.'s goal is to become the first "environmentally restorative" company. Interface has pledged to eliminate any negative impact the company may have had on the environment by 2020. No small feat for a company with manufacturing plants on four continents and annual sales revenue of more than $1 billion. Anderson says on the company web site: "the heart of sustainability is found by making informed choices and gaining the knowledge to act in a way that doesn't jeopardize the future."[14] Interface has maintained its profitability and has been bestowed with numerous awards from "Best Corporate Citizen" to "Best Places to Work," demonstrating that you can have it both ways: You can strive to be a sustainable company and be profitable.

A great question to ask at your next strategic planning or cost-reduction meeting is: How much of our top talent can we recruit because the company is going green? Or how many of the company's top talent will leave because we are not going green?

There is a lot of green (and this time I mean money) to be saved and captured. I love the IBM commercial about energy efficiency.[15] A Generation Y worker brings a green proposal to her skeptical Boomer boss. He believes that "it will make people feel real good about the company and it will go over real well with the tree huggers." He asks her why he should sign this proposal and she explains that the plan would cut energy costs by 40 percent and that the company spent more than $18 million on energy last year. After hearing that, her boss scrambles to figure out where to sign. This great clip gives us a glimpse of not just Generation Y, but what the next generation will bring to our organizations.

My perspective on the future worker is simple and comes from my own experience. I have two young children, and I can tell you that they are keenly aware of environmental issues. Not only do they banter about global warming and how "all the ice could melt" if we don't start taking better care of the Earth, but they understand the need to reduce, reuse and recycle, and how dumping chemicals down the drain can kill ocean life. They are growing up in an age (and are going to be the employees of the future) where there are no "paper or plastic" choices at the grocery store; their only choice is "canvas."

While going green is a factor in building an employment brand for the future, it also applies to retention. Organizations that are not implementing environmental policies or changing the way they're doing business may lose current employees to companies that offer incentives like subsidies for buying hybrid cars, on-site farmers' markets, green commuting vouchers, use of green fuels and solar power — just some of the latest trends in the corporate green scene.

Boston-based EnerNOC helps businesses manage and reduce their electricity consumption. According to David Samuels, senior vice president of Human Resources, "I think now, more than ever before, acting in an environmentally responsible way is top of mind with our employees and potential employees. Our core business is about helping utilities companies think differently about energy consumption, we want to attract and retain employees who share these values."[16]

In brand creation, the key (internal) green recruiting questions that need to be asked and answered are:

■ Is sustainability one of your core organizational values?
  » If so, is it listed on your web site?
■ Do you have an environmental policy?
  » If so, is it posted on your career site?
■ Has your company won any environmental awards?
  » If so, is it posed on your career page?
■ Do you have a recycling program?
  » If so, are you tracking (and communicating) the amount of money you've saved?
  » What about the landfill space you've freed up by doing so?
■ Are you using recyclable stock on your recruiting materials?
■ Have you built in environmental accountability into your performance appraisal system?
■ Do you incentivize employees in any way to support your environmental policies?
■ If your company has a reward system involving redeemable points, do you offer a green option, such as pledged donations to an earth-friendly cause?

The bottom line on going green: Not only is it just the *right* thing to do, but it's a win-win-win — a win for the environment, a win for your employees, and a win for your company's bottom line. Popularity and consciousness around being green is not going away. Your company needs to embrace it as a philosophy and a practiced value in order for you to attract and retain Generation Y and subsequent generations of talented employees.

CHAPTER 9

Combining Culture and Brand in a Merger or Acquisition

Put the M back in M&A

In a true merger, no one culture should win. Having one side win over the other can be the kiss of death to the deal. Unfortunately, more often than not, what I have experienced in the merger frenzy are acquisitions disguised as mergers. There is typically an acquirer and an acquiree, and the lead company's culture typically dominates. If you are the acquiring company in a deal and you are not interested in blending cultures or brand, we hope you will at least respect your partner's culture. Respectfulness helps the "merged" employees see what you as the lead company have to offer in the way of structure, processes, and business behavior. One simple way to accomplish this is to ask people how and why they do the things. It has been my experience that many times a merger/acquisition is met by fear by employees on both sides: They are cautious to talk about the new situation and have an ominous view of things that may come to pass. Deploying a cultural assessment that can be conducted and analyzed in the first 90 days is the key to helping to settle the employee groups, on both sides.

During a merger or acquisition, the elements that make up the acquiring company's culture are being threatened, and the status quo or aspects of the employees' way of life may be changed or, worse yet, lost. The first step in managing a cultural collision is to understand both cultures. You must spend time developing a cultural resume (from both companies), which will support you in creating brand alignment. This process allows you to visualize where there is congruence and incongruence between the two cultures. This process prevents you from blindly jumping into the integration process. Who will be responsible for the cultural integration may be different in each acquisition scenario. This can all be dependent on size, scope, logistics, and national cultural differences. There is not a set formula for the ownership of the integration process, but a good rule of thumb is to create an assimilation team that is comprised of members from both organization and a cross section of senior leadership, Human Resources, line managers, and employees.

Creating a cultural resume for your company and the newly acquired company will also allow you to determine the potential fallout of imposing your culture on your potential partner. This information may cause you to have second thoughts about such an imposition or eliminating a culture that is deep-rooted and successful. There are significant financial gains to be made by organizations that honor those cultural differences and allow the successful company they have just acquired to maintain their culture.

If it isn't Broken, Don't Fix it

Fast Company magazine did a follow-up story from the 1996 merger of IBM (Big Blue) and Tivoli Systems.[1] That article outlined their acquisition approach as: we are not blue, we're not red — we are purple. That was a great positioning statement of how the acquisition would be managed. Big Blue was not going to replace the Tivoli corporate color of red. They wanted to integrate and be purple.

Back in 1996, Big Blue acquired the Austin, Texas-based outfit in hopes of injecting a devotion to speed into a mammoth and often bureaucratic organization. Tivoli excelled in an area that IBM wanted to make its own: software that manages large, dispersed networks, databases, and applications across multiple platforms. Rather than remake Tivoli in its own image, IBM put the Tivoli team in charge of the entire company's systems-management division and granted the group an unusual degree of independence. Tivoli has managed the rare feat of preserving its startup identity even as it became integrated into a larger company. The results were nothing short of dynamic. In 1999, Tivoli remained the fastest-growing division within the IBM software group, with revenues that increased from $1.5 billion to $1.8 billion.

The Tivoli and IBM example is a good reminder to us all that people join organizations for many reasons, but they join the organization, not an organization that might be acquired by the competition. If you wanted to go to work for the competition, you would have done so in the first place. The same can be applied to your employment brand. Brands can be decimated in a merger; they can get watered down or eliminated because your culture is your brand.

You can readily see the obvious extrinsic benefits, but a cultural assessment will help you see the intrinsic cultural benefits: flexible work hours, educational opportunities, casual work environment, the level of trust and empowerment, or the organizational values. The list goes on of what attracted people to your potential partner. Show respect for each other's cultures. They are what brought you to the point of considering and moving forward on this deal.

If you choose the path of cultural assimilation, be aware that you may encounter more negative force and resistance than if you make an effort to work together in building a combined culture.

As a leader, you will begin to see what all engaged couples need to see. The marriage isn't the wedding, nor is the merger the moment you sign all the documents to make it official. Change your focus from getting the deal done to making the partnership viable over the long haul. Understand how to decode and translate the overt messages and publicly available information about your potential partner or your new partner. Unless key players from both organizations learn to read the deeper meanings that the other side's culture communicates, then mutual working relations remain under threat.

Develop a prudent, yet aggressive and solid, transition plan when combining the cultures. The plan must generate a road map outlining what needs to occur by when, and who will make each step happen from the human system integration perspective. Good project management is what I'm talking about. You must be able to measure and track your progress. This cannot occur when you rely on your gut rather than on hard data. A process like cultural due diligence provides you with that data (see Figure 9.1).

Figure 9.1. Cultural Due Diligence and Cultural Health Alignment Process Steps

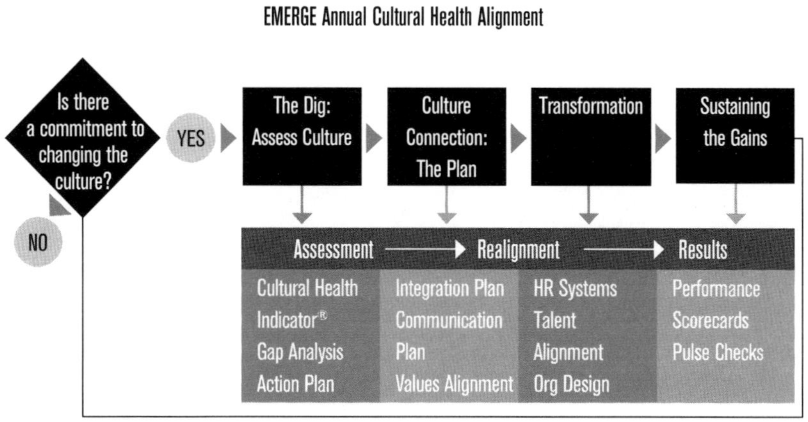

EMERGE Annual Cultural Health Alignment

A classic example took place in the airline industry years ago when US Airways acquired Pacific Southwest Airlines (PSA) in an effort to link its East Coast routes with the markets in the West and Southwest. PSA dominated the California corridor and was one of the first "no frills" airlines. PSA crew members wore casual attire in keeping with the markets they served, and a smile was painted on the nose of each aircraft. In contrast, US Airways, formerly Allegheny Airlines, was one of the oldest national carriers in the country, with a concentration in the Northeast. The primary customers were business travelers, and the management focused on that segment. Before the ink had dried on the contracts, the paintbrushes were wet and employees were busily covering the "smiles." Instead of integrating this favorably viewed aspect of PSA, US Airways literally erased it, along with the culture it represented. In a short period, market share was lost to upstart rival Southwest Airlines, which sensed this cultural incompatibility and took advantage of the opportunity to replace the service that had been lost. Eventually, US Airways all but withdrew from the Southwest, suffering serious financial losses from the cost of the acquisition and the failure to expand its routes. The smiles were gone from everyone's face, especially the shareholders.

So, did US Airways make the same mistake when they combined with America West? No, they did not. Cultural integration became a key factor in making the deal successful. They immediately assigned a Chief Culture Officer, who had a full-time, high-level, highly visible position to integrate the cultures. I'm not saying that this made the transition and integration go off without a hitch. I will say that there were *outward* steps and actions taken that gave us, the humble consumer, a feel that the companies were working hard to come together quickly and effectively. Many travelers like to see the four logos integrated together by the cabin door on every plane. This was not an afterthought. US Airways did this deliberately to show the employees and the public that they were keenly aware of both companies' proud history, including the PSA logo. This was a smart move, albeit a small one, as a way of recognizing and publicizing US Airways' noted shift in their approach to integration, inclusion, and branding.

Honor thy Cross Cultural Differences

As a consultant, I have run across cultural integration issues many times. The inequity (real or perceived), the stepchild mentality, and the utter lack of attention to the W.I.F.M. ("What's In It For Me") issues and cultural differences can be immense. In some cases, I've found that there is a complete disregard for the acquired company's culture.

In 2006, a client was referred to me by a friend who was working with them on process improvement. They had just been acquired by a large British company and were experiencing integration pains, as my friend put it. This company, based in Denver, has less than 100 employees. For the parent company, it was like acquiring a department or a small division. But this little company did something they needed, and they needed it badly. (They manufacture a vital piece of the radiator.)

This company had been owned for decades by the family that founded it and has had multiple generations of the same families working for them for years. Then they were acquired by another large British conglomerate. The new parent company made it clear that they did not want the founding family in the transition plan. They politely created their exit strategy and threw them a big party.

The employees are "salt of the earth" people. They live the Colorado life, really enjoy the outdoors, have a company softball team and bowling league, work hard, play hard, and don't take much gruff from anyone. They have been doing their jobs just fine for years and didn't take kindly to new people entering their "family," let alone being the new boss of it. But, in the infinite wisdom of the new parent company, they felt this would be an outstanding stretch assignment for a high potential they had their eye on for the past few years. So, enter the new CEO, spouting off "Brilliant!" and "Hey mate!" to everyone she passed.

The British conglomerate wanted to integrate the employees quickly. They wanted to get everyone on board and make the Colorado employees feel like they were part of the team. So they shipped over printed safety standards, printed vision, mission, values posters, and their cute little company mascot-adorned tea mugs (all stamped "Made in England" on the bottom). The mascot looked very similar to the American cartoon character Bob the Builder. The stated company values are also printed on the mugs. The values read like this:

- Commitment — Never doing less than you can
- Delivery — If you promise to do something, do it
- Winning — Achieving in spite of; not failing because of
- Respect — Recognising and acknowledging the contribution of others

Taken as a stand-alone, these four values aren't bad — they're standard corporate values. The insult to injury here is the fact that this "salt of the earth" U.S. workforce is part of an industry that truly believes in the "buy American" philosophy. The "Made in England" mugs were a bit of a misstep but the blatant British spelling of *recognising* (as opposed to *recognizing*) was the proverbial kiss of death. From the start, the CEO knew she was going to have a cultural integration nightmare on her hands. She knew that, as a woman from the United Kingdom, she was going to have a hard time fitting in with her employees. But, she also knew enough about human relationships, human interaction, and honoring the human spirit to understand that as soon as the "brass" went back to the UK, she was going to conduct a cultural assessment to figure out, quantitatively, exactly what was going on. She was going to extend a metaphorical olive branch, be herself, be honest, be authentic, and give resources and time to allow for an evolution of change to take place, not a revolution of change. Luckily for the British parent company and the radiator parts company, they had an evolved leader who realized when to step back and honor the system holistically — all of the people, practices, and systems that she had just come to be in charge of.

Over the years of working with clients, I have seen many companies that have not taken the time to understand the national (even regional) cultural differences that today's mergers and acquisitions face. Instead, they choose to operate with the philosophy, "Damn the torpedoes — full speed ahead!"

In most acquisitions it is difficult, if not impossible, to contact the *to be acquired* companies employees before the deal is done. This road block sets up the need to conduct an early and thorough assessment of organizational culture, which can help the acquiring company forecast the deal and manage cultural issues before they become bottlenecks and diminish deal value.

Following a merger, people stay where they are for many reasons, and people leave jobs for many reasons, but when it comes to cultural integration, you need to have a back-up plan and not assume the majority of A-level players are going to stick around if you start changing their culture. If the culture is no longer "what they signed up for," they are the ones who will move on. They can get a job just about anywhere.

In *Managing Mergers and Acquisitions*,[2] the authors comment on the classic book *In Search of Excellence*,[3] saying:

> Tom Peters and Bob Waterman presented clear evidence linking
> organizational performance with a strong, dominant and coherent culture.
> Although the level of performance of several of the "excellent" companies
> has declined in the years since the study, this does not weaken the argument
> that a fragmented, ambiguous or contradictory culture is unlikely to result in
> optimum organizational performance. The organizational performance of even
> "excellent" companies is likely to decline if they are unable either to continue
> to maintain a cohesive culture or to recognize the need to change.

The role of a cultural diagnostic process

When trying to diagnose the cause of the alarmingly high rate of failures (measured in terms of reported financial performance compared with projected revenues), many people are looking to the cultural issues. In an article in *Modern Healthcare*, Rodney Fralicz and C.J. Bolster state that "Culture can be a make-or-break factor in the merger equation, which, if ignored or misunderstood, can almost single-handedly sour the deal."[4]

In *Organizational Culture and Leadership*, Edgar H. Schein states,

> Culture may be loosely thought about, but it is only after the merger that it is
> taken seriously, suggesting that most leaders make the assumption that they
> can fix cultural problems after the fact. I would argue that leaders must make

cultural analysis as central to the initial merger/acquisition decision as is the financial, product, or market analysis.[5]

Schein goes on to point out that mistakes in this area can be costly. He offers the example of a U.S. company that was about to be acquired by a larger British firm. The company actually conducted an internal audit of its own culture and concluded that being taken over by this firm would not be palatable. The company waited for a more attractive partner to come along. A French company that was *perceived* to be a better cultural match entered the picture. The U.S. company had not conducted a formal cultural audit of this firm. The decision to move forward was based strictly on perception. The U.S. company was purchased by the French firm, and, six months later, the French parent sent over a management team that decimated the U.S. company and imposed processes that were much less compatible with the U.S. company's culture than anything its executives could ever have imagined. But it was too late!

Figure 9.2 is a good guide post to use, post M&A, to ensure there is a strategic approach and strategic plan to integrate the human system.

Figure 9.2. Post Deal Assessment Guide

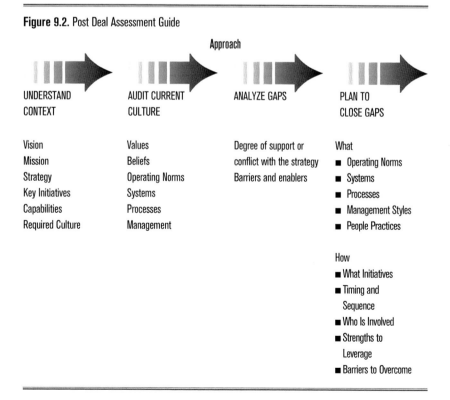

Approach

UNDERSTAND CONTEXT	AUDIT CURRENT CULTURE	ANALYZE GAPS	PLAN TO CLOSE GAPS
Vision	Values	Degree of support or	What
Mission	Beliefs	conflict with the strategy	■ Operating Norms
Strategy	Operating Norms	Barriers and enablers	■ Systems
Key Initiatives	Systems		■ Processes
Capabilities	Processes		■ Management Styles
Required Culture	Management		■ People Practices

How
■ What Initiatives
■ Timing and
  Sequence
■ Who Is Involved
■ Strengths to
  Leverage
■ Barriers to Overcome

Case in Point: Merging Cultures

In 1995, I was assigned to my first acquisition and cultural integration project. I know many professionals who have shared very similar stories with me and the take away learning from experiences like this is you must take the time to learn the culture of the company you are acquiring. While this may not be able to be done in a formal due diligence until right after the deal is done, there is cursory research you can do to find out about what it is like to work there. It was this experience that helped to create a tool called The Brand Scan (covered in Chapter 10). The company I was working for at the time, an East Coast medical supply manufacturing company with more than 2,000 employees, acquired a small (40 person) technology company in Bothell, Wash. Geographic differences were apparent from the start, but the fundamental business and technology were closely aligned. The marching orders were to head out to Bothell and let the employees know who they were. Share benefit information, salary structure, and position expectations. Take time to outline all the information and get back to the East Coast with signed letters of employment agreements or consulting contracts to manage the intellectual property transfer.

The team flew to Seattle, all suited up for the meeting. Suited up is the operative word here; we took no time to try and understand the culture we were walking into. The differences were apparent from the start: While we were in suits, everyone there was dressed in blue jeans, boots, and sweaters. We spent the day with the employees going over the typical transition plan information and assumed they would all want to come to work for us. We gave them 24 hours to read the packages and come back with a signed offer. The outcome was that no one was willing to consider relocation, let alone help in the transfer of knowledge if it involved having to travel to the East Coast. Please don't think that the suits and blue jeans was the shocking cultural difference that created this situation. It is much deeper than that. But the dress code is only one indication of behavioral differences. There were significant differences in the incentive programs, flexibility in work schedules, work/life balance, and, yes, climate. Everyone lives somewhere for a reason, and for companies to assume that the newly acquired employees are going to pack up and move to keep their jobs is not a good strategic approach to acquisition.

I learned that while the integration of IT, communication, payroll, and finance systems are vitally important to a successful deal, the deal may not be successful if you don't have the employees, the people, the humans (the *human system*) involved or integrated right from the start. Employment brand and cultural integration go hand in hand. You will have to retrofit brand post M&A, but if you keep it simple, and keep it aligned to vision, mission, and values, you will attain a higher rate of success.

CHAPTER 10

The Employment Branding Tool Kit: How to Build a Brand

This chapter is dedicated to bring ideas, tips, and structure to the process of creating an employment brand. From what we have reviewed, you may already be "thinking like a marketer" and pulling the puzzle pieces together on how to get started in brand creation.

Asking the Right Questions

Before getting started on a branding effort, there are steps to follow and key questions that need to be answered about your organization. Use these questions as a checklist to ensure you have developed a foundation and plan for the employment branding effort.

Sponsorship

- Do we have senior-level support for the employment branding activity?
- Do we have funding? If so, how much budget has been allocated? And have we broken that down into "buckets" in order to see where we can contract with externals or have to do the work internally?
- Have we used the "productivity calculator" to establish the potential productivity loss from disengagement? Have we developed charts and graphs for the senior leadership team?
- What is the chain of command in brand creation? And who will have final-signature authority on what to spend?

Data Collection and Metrics for Calculating ROI

- Have we gathered enough information from a valid sample of our employee population pursuant to what our culture is and is not?
- Can we use data we have already collected in our employee satisfaction surveys or employee engagement studies to serve as a baseline for understanding our true organizational culture in order to build an authentic and congruent brand?

- Have we validated our mission, vision, and values against what the employees understand to be our mission and hold as a value themselves? (Note: This is where the quick-gap analysis and values exercise located in Chapter 4 would come in very handy.)
- Have we defined our values in behavioral terms and tied them to our EVP?
- What metrics are we going to create or deploy to track the ROI of our efforts?

The EVP and Generational Differences

- When was the last time we looked at our EVP? Do we even have one? What will it take to create one? Will we need external support to determine this before beginning brand creation?
- What are our generational differences? Do we have a multi-generational workforce we will be working to attract, retain, and repel, or are we in an area or industry that will cater to one demographic sort more than another?

External Forces

- Are there any external considerations we should forecast before starting down the path? Are there plans for mergers, divestitures, or downsizing that would affect the message of the brand?
- Has there been any negative press in relation to how the company has "responded vs. reacted" that may need to be countered or addressed in the creation of brand? If so, assuming you have a PR or communication plan, can your team develop messaging to counter any negative press?
- What are the company's plans of environmental sustainability? This will come into play as external forces: customers, shareholders, and potential employees, as well as internal forces such as your current customers, employees, and vendors.
- Have we conducted an in-depth review of your competitor's web site and found relevant information to leverage or counter?

Branding Team and Vendor Selection

- What is the time frame to pull a branding team together?
- What is the composite of this team? (The steps for this process were covered in the marketing chapter.)
- Have we made the determination of the use of strictly internal resources or external vendors, or a blend of resources that will be used? If choosing external resources, what will the process be to identify the vendor of choice? This may have to include an RFP process, which will push out our time frame for delivery and budget.

■   If choosing an external resource, will it be a blend of companies with specific core competencies or one vendor that can provide all the support? This again may affect the budget and RFP process. If you have a short window or time frame for brand creation, consider using smaller firms that can bring all the pieces to you without having to go through the RFP process or pay large agency fees.

Creative and Emotional Messaging

The next step is to look at the emotional and technical components of employment brand creation. The emotional or creative side is important, as pointed out in the Liberty Mutual example in Chapter 3. The path you take here can create a *movement* for not only your employees; it also can help you find a customer base you have not reached out to in the past and could have a direct, positive impact on your ROI.

The creative side has to tie into this emotional side of the brand, and they have to play well together. In branding, nothing can be done as a stand-alone step. This is why developing a well thought out plan (identifying both internal and external resources) before getting started is a key piece to the planning phase. In the development of your employment brand, one of the first steps to take is the development of the Brand Promise statement. A promise statement is like an EVP, but it is condensed into a promise or statement of what you (the company) will give, what the employee will get, and what is expected in return.

When you and your team (internal or external) have agreed on the Brand Promise statement, then all communication materials from offer letters, benefit information, recruitment fair fliers, termination letters, and severance packages need to be expressed following the employment brand communication guidelines set out in the creative process. Make sure that this process factors in compliance with HR policy and relevant federal, state, and local laws. You want to keep in mind the sage Total Quality Management advice — "consistency is quality" — and follow that closely. Color and aesthetics play a crucial role in the success of materials and have been used wisely by marketers in the development of brand identification. While consumers may forget a specific brand name, they will likely remember the color associated with the product.

One of the best ways to create your outline for an effective employment brand is to evaluate other companies' web sites and marketing communication. In the evaluation step of a competitor, one way to judge if the brand is effective is if it elicits an emotional response. Does it move you into action? Do you feel anything when you see the brand? Does it make you laugh?

Procter & Gamble (P&G) is an excellent example of a large global company that has created an experience on their site (www.pgjobs.com). The first thing to note is the web address. It is important to secure www.yourcompanyname.jobs. While P&G does a good job of using "jobs" in the link, the growing trend for companies is to purchase www.yourcompanyname.jobs. If you don't, someone else will, and, in the future, you may have to pay to recapture your own company name. The .jobs tag helps you move up on search engines. It also secures your name and directs job seekers to your site — the site you want them to go to and not one that is unauthorized by your company.

The second important feature of the P&G site is the video and animation. The P&G animated video is outstanding because it conveys a message from start to finish in 40 seconds — a very short time, which holds your interest. The music is moving, uplifting, yet not overly familiar. The characters in the video are very diverse and appear to be supporting each other. The video starts and ends with the same word, *Challenge*, which allows for the mental connection. The dots (or bubbles) move across the screen, into a conference room, over each employee's head, giving us the sensation of innovative and creative thinking, then take us through familiar brands while standing at our own kitchen sink. We can connect with brand names like Pampers and Swiffer. Once their consumer brand is established, they move on to the part where it shows the characters helping each other move boxes in a way that conveys servitude. It gives you the feeling the characters are helping people who need help, which establishes a socially responsible theme. The last movement is the blinking dots pointing to their company locations around the globe. The final shot ends with the words, "Discover your challenge, Discover your future." You have an experience in those 40 seconds, and the video spot ends with a statement that supports what you have just watched:

> A career at P&G offers a chance to touch someone's life. Our people get involved — with their workplace, their community, their neighbors and each other. If you want a company whose actions reflect their ethics and whose people live their values, then you should consider a career at P&G.

Another feature on this site is they have links on the page that will engage the potential job seeker into finding out more about "what the culture is like, what it would really be like to work here." And they brilliantly cover the ability to "attract" employees.

Once you have identified a web site or a brand that is appealing to you, now look at the similarities in your organization to the brand you have found. Can you tie any of the creative into your own brand while keeping it authentic and real to your organizational culture?

There are more than a quarter of a billion web sites to "shop" among. Everyone has a web site these days — it is today's calling card. John Sullivan emphasizes the need for having a strong career site as part of your overall web site strategy, and that careers site needs to be connected, with purpose, and that is congruent and authentic.

> These web sites are bad, most to the point of embarrassment. When will companies realize that whatever employment branding or advertising you do is instantly lost when 70% of your applicants judge the credibility of what you said based on what they find on your website? Without exception, candidates find dated material, dinosaur technology and copy that's about as exciting as reading an accounting textbook.[1]

No offense to accounting textbook authors, but Sullivan is exactly right. Dull, dated, and directionless is neither an effective web strategy nor a winning employer branding campaign.

Your career site is the first step in achieving the Attract, Retain, Repel goal. It begins with ensuring your message is a true expression of your organizational culture and viewed as a positive that can increase the ROI of your recruitment and retention activities.

In a November 7, 2008, presentation to the Texas Association of Health Care Recruiters, Matthew Adam of NAS Recruitment Communication said that there are usually four main barriers to building a great web site. I have added my parenthetical take on these steps as it relates to my approach.

1. *Speed of change.* (The world is changing so fast and businesses are shifting at such great speeds. This that means your web site should be designed to allow for maximum flexibility for modifications.)

2. *Resources.* (Do you have the internal resources to create a great site or would your IT department see this as a check box on the checklist and not give it the full attention it requires?)

3. *Know how.* (Has branding been a past core competency or have you involved the consumer marketing representatives. Brand is not something to just make up, so having the knowledge and skills is a must-have.)

4. *Ownership.* (Who will own the branding process? Dedicating resources to monitor brand and messaging is a pivotal step in the process.)

These are great points and ones that need to be addressed in the design and planning stage of web site development. However, I would add a pre-step here that has to do with the vision of the career site.

There are a lot of technical and logistical pieces that go into career site development and brand creation, but having the vision for what you are attempting to create is the first step to take before you begin to design, shift, or change your current brand and message.

One of the first indicators of a good career site is that it has an easy navigation system. I call this the "three clicks and you're out" rule. If a potential job seeker cannot find your career site and plug in the desired job or position in three clicks (a click is defined as how many times you have to touch your mouse or keys to move on to the next page of the site or step in the job search process), then they will probably move on. While there may not be statistics that support our "three click" rule, it is intuitive that the longer it takes to find what you are looking for, the less likely you will stick with the search. You can also get the job seeker who is truly interested in your company; they may stick around for up to five clicks, but more than five clicks and the average page visitor is bored. And think of it from their perspective: What does a cumbersome, hard-to-navigate career site say about the culture of your organization? If the first interaction a candidate has with your organization is one of frustration, they may not have the patience to continue looking for a job, but they may also create a perception that the organization is rigid or tough to interact with.

I have seen an interesting trend developing on job postings in the first quarter of 2009. Companies are beginning to list their values on the first page of the resume submission process. It is much like a gate keeper step where you are asked to read the values and determine whether or not you agree with them. This is a very exacting question and approach to cultural fit. If you accept them, you have to click a button and then proceed with the application submission If you do not agree with them, and do not click the accept button, you are done. There is not an option for you to continue unless you have agreed to and accepted the organizational values. This approach is a perfect example of how to repel an employee who will not fit.

Case in Point: Name That Company

Which company...

- Gets 1,300 unsolicited resumes *a day*?
- Is not just on *Fortune*'s "100 Best Places to Work" list, but tops it?
- Is now a common verb in the *Oxford Dictionary*?

Give up? It's Google!
In 2005, Google posted a "day in the life of a Googler" video on its web site. Although the video was long, it gave viewers an in-depth look at what

is was like to experience a Google day. This virtual-tour approach allows candidates to make an informed choice on the organization based on what they see, not only on what they can hear or read about a company.

The bottom line: Innovative companies are innovative in attracting job seekers.

Unfortunately, most company web sites (including their career pages) do not use their actual employees. Instead, they use stock house images with generic models. This approach simply does not convey an authentic reality that today's job seeker is looking for. What do these stock employees (or worse, those sites that just show buildings) say about your culture? Certainly not that people are your most valuable asset! Many companies want to convey that they value diversity and have a family environment, but you can do this without the stock photos. The most powerful message will come from real people — your real people.

This is a new and exciting period in which digital technologies have finally become affordable. And video is the most powerful way for your company to convey its culture.

Why is video so important to your employment brand? Peter Weddle stated that,

> … the old advertising truism that a person had to see a commercial seven times for it to break through his or her consciousness, now it might take 70 times for a message to break through.[2]

Consider these facts about online videos:[3]

- 52 percent of all Internet traffic is driven by online video.
- More than 70 percent of all Internet users watch videos online.
- 123 million Americans watched videos online during every single month of 2007.
- Because online video is so popular, the Big 3 search engines — Google, Yahoo!, and MSN — comb the video web sites every few minutes looking for fresh content.
- Video content can show up in the search results within just a few hours of an article being uploaded to any video web site.
- Video content frequently shows up in the search results ahead of other types of content.
- When Cisco added streaming video to its web site, the traffic to its web site increased by 600 percent.

Robert Rosell, president of Quality Media Resources, said, "Gen Y is a generation that is used to a lot of entertainment. They multitask; they do a lot of things at once. They're perfectly comfortable watching a stream video on their computer while they're texting with their left hand and writing a report with their right."[4] Video is natural to the younger generations; they are familiar with it and expect it. A good example of this is what the military has done with their brand on the web and on television. They offer video games on their site so the potential applicant can play a "real game" to see what it might be like in that branch of the service. This approach is in support of the process of attract and repel.

The cost of video for your web site can vary significantly from a do it yourself with a Flip video camera ($195), or home shot production that includes editing ($2,500-$5,000), to a professional, cinematic creation, which can run anywhere from $15,000 to $25,000, depending on number of locations and filming options. This cost does not include the creative development or typical advertising agency fees. Those can run more than $100,000.

But a note of caution: Don't just shoot a video just to post a video. It will not come across as authentic and can eventually come back to haunt you, as can a "company song" that usually comes off as cheesy or contrived. Today's video technology has been simplified. The average user can interface, understand, and apply it. It is not unheard of for a company to purchase an off-the-shelf video camera and walk around and videotape employees and the workplace. The challenge is to ensure the video is an accurate, authentic, and congruent depiction of your organizational culture.

If you want to collect *real stories* from *real people*, consider podcasts. Many people may already own an iPod. For $89.00, you can purchase a Bilkin microphone that snaps on the top and allows you to record hours of voice memos, interviews, music, etc. Once you have created the recording, you can upload this to your iTunes and transfer to your web site. Some organizations are using their CEOs to record a message that speaks from the top of the leadership ranks to perspective and current employees. Podcasts are a very effective way to communicate information and allows for maximum flexibility as they can be accessed at any time by hundreds of users. Let's say you take the "man on the street approach" and walk around your organization and ask the question, "So, what is it really like to work here?" You might be surprised at the information and stories you gather. Plus, you can always delete what doesn't work well. It is a good idea to try both the planned sit down interview and the walk-by approach as they will gather different voices and copy for you to choose from.

Shoba Purushothaman, CEO of The NewsMarket, offers sound, cost-effective, and powerful advice on how to reach a wide audience.[5]

1. Shoot video that will work with all media. When embarking on a video shoot, make sure it's the highest broadcast quality. You might want to use this outside of the web, so don't limit your options by using streaming video only.
2. Images speak louder than words, so make sure you use images that tell a story. And articulate the benefits of what you are promoting.
3. Choose an off-the-shelf video solution instead of having your IT teams build something from scratch.
4. Make it "sharable." Today's consumer wants to share and interact with content, so make sure your video can be e-mailed, linked to, embedded in blogs, and that journalists can easily gain access to high-quality versions. By making it easy for others to spread messages for you, you will increase your reach exponentially. There may be intellectual property and privacy issues in play here but for now sharing on the web remains to be the wild west of olden days.

R.L. Polk & Co. has a webpage with employees standing in line. First thing you notice is that they all look engaged. You can click on any employee and their picture turns to face you; they tell you who they are in written form. No expensive video, just copy and a photo shoot. Under the photograph, they describe what the company is and who the people on the team are. The header is "Why Polk is a cool place to work." There do not appear to be any technical issues related to the mouse-over with each employee. The site works well without the large spend on creative. They make the case that:

> Your opportunity for career growth is as unlimited as your imagination, passion, creativity and dedication. Polk understands the value of its employees and provides competitive salaries, coupled with contemporary benefit programs to assure a sound financial future for its workforce. Polk is an equal opportunity employer dedicated to embracing diversity and committed to attracting and retaining bright, talented, skilled individuals who desire to be a part of today's fastest growing information industry.[6]

No need to reinvent the wheel. You can find outstanding web-worthy copy that is already written. It might take you some time in research and honing your search skills, but there is unlimited information that can be repackaged and is a good fit for your organization. You cannot take someone's copy as your own, so ensure you rework the copy to make it relevant to your organization and to ensure that it isn't plagiarism.

There are also web sites that are leveraging video technology for job hunters and corporate recruiters. Some are adding online video resumes to their offerings. I have found three that are worth taking a look at.

1. *WorkBlast.* Job seekers create a free profile page that can be viewed. They can send the video to as many e-mail contacts as they choose. Employers pay to subscribe.
2. *Mypersonalbroadcast.* Essentially the same service but they provide tracking metrics to who watched the individual's video. It is popular with college students.
3. *HireVue.* Works much like a virtual interview site and helps reduce costs in flying candidates in for interviews. Employer's direct candidates to the site and give them a pass code, where they are asked specific questions. They are given two minutes to answer while videotaping their answers. This option is cost-effective and supportive of sustainability practices.

Global Messaging and Selling a Lifestyle

An important step in message creation is the special care global companies must take in brand creation or message creation. You must ensure that, if you are global and reaching out to a diverse and multi-lingual population, you use the "local language" and not just something a professional translation company can pull together for you. Ensure a local language speaker reviews the survey questions or message you create before launching any campaign. There have been numerous marketing case studies that remind us that choice of language and words play a critical role on how our products are received in another country. The car company Chevrolet made one mistake with the Chevy Nova. They did not test or review the product name translation. Nova loosely translates to "won't go" in Spanish, which created a difficult time tapping into the Spanish-speaking market.

International companies must consider how to sell a lifestyle or expatriate assignment. We know that language, both written and verbal, is a key medium for communicating marketing messages, and the same goes for employment branding. It is an essential characteristic that can differentiate one culture from another — and even one subculture from another within an organization.

Case in Point: Saudi Aramco

Saudi Aramco is an international company whose challenge in the attract phase of recruiting is to "sell a lifestyle," not just a job.[7] When you are considering employment with this company, it requires you to move to Saudi Arabia. This presents a unique challenge to their organization.

Here is how the Saudi Aramco page opens:

LIFESTYLE

If you're thinking of joining us, you probably have plenty of questions. What is it like to live here? What about the communities, the type of housing, the quality of the schools and the availability of recreational facilities?

Well, we have good news. Most of the community and residential services are provided at no charge. Buses, schools, maintenance and use of athletic facilities are free. Even electricity, water and local telephone services are free. And there's lots more besides.

They then go into a description of every facet of "life" you might have questions about – everything from transportation to health care to food shopping. I was amazed at what the company had to do to not only "sell the job" but sell where you would be living, how you would live, and what you may encounter and or experience.

COMMUNITY LIFE

Saudi Aramco communities are comprised of housing similar to parts of the U.S. southwest with tree-lined streets, grass lawns, schools, grocery stores and golf courses, swimming pools and a host of other athletic and community facilities. Residents can walk, ride bicycles or take a bus almost anywhere they want to go. The company designed, developed and continues to operate these communities specifically for its employees.

Their web site is a good example of specific messaging you may have to create and how to frame it so the candidate will understand "what they will experience" from the lifestyle vantage point.

Case in Point: Kennedy Information

One way to frame the experience is to provide information on how the employee population at your organization is both similar and different (diverse). A good example of this is on the Kennedy Information web site.[8]

On the opening page, there is standard information on the company: Founded in 1970 by James Kennedy, Kennedy Information is a leading source of research, news, and information for professionals in the Management and IT Consulting, Executive Recruiting, and Investor Relations professions. Additionally, the company provides a variety of career services for job seekers at the professional and executive level.

The next section is where they outline "what they are." In this section, you can imagine a prospective candidate saying, "Hey, I like to do those things too!" This speaks to attract but also to retain. Basically, the candidate can picture spending a fair amount of time with co-workers who share similar interests.

We Are:

Skiers, Gourmet Chefs, Justices of the Peace, Webheads, Dead-heads, Cliff Divers, Fast Drivers, Barristers, Sailors, Fathers, Moth-ers, Train Buffs, Hockey Players, Bass Guitar Players, Gardeners, Hikers, Mountain Bikers, Dee Jays, Food Aficionados, Novelists, Tae-Kwon-Do Aerobics Fans, Cribbage Players, MBAs, Antique Collectors, Skeptics, Astronomers, Grandparents, Gamblers, War Gamers, Horseback Riders, Quilters, Golfers, Coffee Addicts, Clowns, Jazz Fans, Community Volunteers, Snowmobile Riders, Pool Players, Photographers, Dorothy Parker Fans, Travelers, Snowshoers, Military Historians, Cancer Survivors, Racquetball Players, Runners, Wine Collectors, BBQ Enthusiasts, Vegetarians, Painters, Croquet Players, Youth Soccer Coaches, Dog Lovers, Teachers, U.S. History Buffs, Bikers, Triathletes, Ruggers, Indie Rockers, Football Players, Baseball Players, Knitters, Massage Therapists, RVers, Dog Enthusiasts, Trekkiers, Gummy Bear Connoisseurs, Cave Explorers, Authors, Alpaca Farmers, Dog Breeders, Sky Divers, Fathers of Teenagers, Sponge Bob Fans, Wiffleball Players, Film Buffs, Scout Leaders, Scrapbookers.

In the next two sections, they outline where they went to college and also some of the organizations the employees have worked for, prior to being at Kennedy. You can assume that a potential job seeker who may have gone to one of these schools might take a few minutes to head to their alumni directory and look up Kennedy Information to see if any of their classmates work there. Or, someone might take a moment to get onto LinkedIn and try and search their old employer to find a shared experience. Again, the emotional connection or personal affiliation can be leveraged as a big draw.

While the Kennedy site isn't too high-tech, they do a good job of stating what they are and what the people are like that work there. Subtle ways of conveying information can be as powerful as flashy sites and high-tech operations. This really does go back to cultural fit, what the job seeker is looking for, and what you really offer in your EVP.

In web site development to communicate your message, there are a couple of "must haves" for your site.

One problem with many web sites is that the career information or link is not in the top navigation bar of the page. This link should not be buried at the foot of your page, where one has to scroll down to find it. If it is easy to see, it's more inviting. This is where HR, IT, marketing, and the senior leadership might have the biggest challenge in reaching agreement on site design, as most company web sites are consumer-driven.

Customer-driven sites are important; you want your customers to go there and buy something or better understand your products and services. The home page, or main site, is not usually designed as a career site. But, you must use your home page to direct, guide, or help the job seeker not only find you, but search for a job. My advice is to work with an external vendor for the technical side of web site development, as they will have the KSAs and data on other client sites that have been successful. You can attend webinars on Search Engine Optimization (SEO) or Search Engine Marketing (SEM), which will give you a good base line of understanding. When using any SEO/SEM service provider, ask if they have SEO experts. Like recruiting, there is no barrier to entry for SEO professionals; you don't want to find yourself working with an inexperienced provider. A bad SEO strategy can be detrimental to your success.

You can also check out services like Jobs2web (which will take your career site outside of your fire wall and unleash your job content on Google), Indeed, and Simply Hired. This gets you exposure and offers a way to get around any IT or firewall challenges you may have.

Another company to check out is Arbita. Their new approach to bundling services is cost-effective, and they may be the next generation of employment branding and recruitment companies. If you want the job seeker to find you quickly and be able to search job openings fast, remember the "three click and you are out rule." You don't want the candidate to have to enter information for

15 to 20 minutes. You want to allow them to upload a resume quickly, and you want to arrange for that resume to "go somewhere." Arbita.net works on both the front and back ends. All the analytics comes from job boards. The landing pages for job postings and the search engine pay-per-click (PPC) ads streamline the application process, while delivering the data that the company's applicant tracking system (ATS) needs. Appealing site content/functionality like video, job search agents, and RSS feeds are valuable for branding, but the most important element is a quick-apply process. Together, the improved candidate experience dramatically reduces the abandonment rate of prospective applicants that ATS' often suffer (analogous to the abandoned shopping cart in the e-commerce world). All that data automatically rolls up into reports. As a result, the company removes the guesswork from their recruitment marketing and branding spending; they know which channels deliver the best candidates for each type of job requisition.

Your career site should also include your job descriptions, but not just position descriptions. You should tie your EVP right into the job description. This is an integral part of the employment branding process. You are trying to create an experience, but if your job postings are dry, formal, and only hit the corporate speak, you may miss out on candidates who might go to an organization that they feel they connect with. Think of your job descriptions as more of an invitation to join your workforce. Ensure you are editing your job postings. Would you send a wedding invitation out that had typos, misspelling, or misinformation attached? Typos convey a poor image of your company. Keep in mind, you want the "A" players to apply, but if these players do not see your company as the best place to work, they may not stop to apply.[9]

Your career section is a good place to post your vision, mission, and values. The values of the company should not be listed like a laundry list. They must communicate what those values *mean* to the organization.

Case in Point: AMD's Vision, Mission, and Values[10]

Vision
A world where the amazing power of AMD technology improves the quality of people's lives.

Mission
Lead through innovative, customer-centric solutions that empower businesses, enhance the digital lifestyle and bridge the digital divide.

Values & Beliefs

AMD's culture is characterized by an indomitable will to succeed and prosper in one of the world's most challenging industries. At the heart of our unique and strong culture is the belief that people are the ultimate source of our competitive advantage. By living these core values, each one of us helps to deliver on our promises to customers, maximize shareholder value and ensure our enduring success.

Respect for People

We respect people, honor diversity and treat each other fairly. These are the cornerstones of our culture and key to our ability to work successfully as a global team.

Integrity

We operate with the highest standards of honesty and responsibility – as individuals and as a corporation – to be a role model worldwide through our business practices, community involvement and environmental stewardship.

Our Customers' Success

We ensure our customers' continuous success by forging deep relationships founded on our commitment to meet their diverse technology needs and a shared passion for excellence.

Customer-Centric Innovation

We lead through innovation – championing creative ideas and solutions that enable our customers to truly differentiate their solutions in the marketplace.

Initiative & Accountability

We deliver on our promises to our customers, stakeholders and to each other by taking risks, seeking proactive solutions and assuming ownership of the results.

Fair & Open Competition

We believe that fair and open competition places the freedom of choice in the hands of customers, allowing the widest population to have access to the best possible technology.

Awards, Rewards, and Recognition

People want to work for winners. If your company has won any kind of award in the past few years, put it on a banner or bar on your career site. This lets candidates know you are noted and recognized for something great. Many organizations that have been on the *Fortune* "100 Best Companies to Work For" list know how to leverage this recognition.

Many of the winners know that this is a prestigious award and can (and will) attract candidates. There are other awards that are not as well known, but most prominent magazines run an annual contest and seek to choose the employer of choice or employer of excellence related to their content (see Table 10.1). If you have not recently won an award, apply for one sooner rather than later to stay ahead of your competition.

Table 10.1. Magazines that Run "Best" Contests

HR Magazine publishes the Annual SHRM/Great Place to Work® Institute Best Small and Medium Companies to Work for in America.
Published by *Fortune Magazine* but administered by Hewitt Associates and The RBL Group, this list focuses on best leadership.
Business Week publishes a list to be on if you want to attract the best people graduating from high school or college.
Consulting Magazine publishes the top 10 consulting companies to work for.
Working Mother Magazine is targeted at working women, and it highlights the many benefits that women-friendly companies offer.
National Geographic offers the top 50 places to live and play; you can leverage your location if it appears on the list. While not something your company has won, it is a good public relations approach.
The business journal in your own home town may run the best places to work on a local level.

Case in Point: W.L. Gore and Associates

W.L. Gore and Associates in Wilmington, Delaware, is one example of how companies can craft the honor of being on the *Fortune* list into a career message and ensure that it is front and center on their *home page* and career page.[11]

Explore Careers at Gore

Do you welcome challenge, personal growth, and the freedom to in-novate in an entrepreneurial environment?

Our associates consistently call Gore a great place to work. Find out why in our Careers section, explore the opportunities available at Gore worldwide, and apply on line.

Gore Again Named to *FORTUNE* List

For the twelfth consecutive year, Gore has been named to *FOR-TUNE*'s list of "100 Best Companies to Work For." Read the related press release.

Social Networking and Web 2.0

New technologies have transformed the strategies we use to find talent. Web 2.0 and social networks have changed the way we communication and interact.

How we speak, and the terms we use, have changed. You will need to keep current in support your branding efforts (see Table 10.2), and you will want to stay as relevant as you can in this dynamic time of change and transition. This is not to only attract Generation Y and the Next Gen; we see a continued trend where all generations are getting web savvy. While I don't have statistics on this, I just have to look at the e-mails my 77-year-old mother sends me to assume she is spending a lot of time online and has created a good skill for research and use of technology.

Table 10.2. Some of the Current Terminology

Aggregation/Aggregator: Collating information from multiple web sources, often done via RSS (or ATOM). Aggregation combines information from multiple sources and republishes it in a unified location.

Blog: A web-based journal created by single or multiple writers

Blogosphere: Referring to the whole world of blogs, inclusive of all kind of communities where people engage in blogging.

Blogroll: A list of a blogger's cohorts, peers, or other bloggers they read and/or recommend. The list usually appears on the left or right sidebar of a blog. Derived from political logrolling where legislators promise votes for each other's bills, implying that bloggers typically only link to blogs who link back to them.

IM: Instant messaging or "chatting" online using tools such as Windows Live Messenger, AOL Instant Messenger, Yahoo! Messenger, Google Talk, Skype, etc.

continued on next page

Table 10.2. Some of the Current Terminology (continued)

Instant Messaging: Real-time conversation between two or more people

Mashup: Similar to aggregation, but more of a web application hybrid that combines functionality from two or more web services to create a whole new application.

Newsreader: A desktop or online tool that "reads" or collects RSS feeds (see below). A feed is a published RSS or ATOM web address to which newsreaders subscribe.

Podcast: A blog of audio (or sometimes video) broadcasts. You can listen to a podcast on any computer or via a large number of portable devices and Mp3 players including but not limited to iPods.

RSS: Real Simple Syndication allows subscriber to receive automatic updates whenever new content is added (think Twitter.)

SaaS: Software as a service. Software delivered over the Internet (as opposed to on your desktop) and to which you purchase a subscription on some kind of monthly or other regular basis (such as every quarter or every year.) Sometimes also referred to as hosted software. Leading analysts such as Gartner are predicting that within a few years over 25 percent of business applications will be delivered as a SaaS model vs. traditional licensing.

Search Engine Optimization (SEO): Part of an overall web marketing strategy, this is the process of improving the quantity and quality of traffic coming to your web site from search engines.

Social Bookmarking: Storing and often sharing links to your favorite web sites (also called Bookmarks) in an online collaborative platform (i.e., del.icio.us or Furl).

Social Networks: Web-based services that allow users to create online communities (for example, Facebook, MySpace, YouTube, Ning, and LinkedIn)

Tags: Keywords that describe the content of a web site, bookmark, photo, or blog post.

Widgets: Small applications that run on your computer or web site and help integrate you or your web site with Social Media and other "Web 2.0" technologies. If it can be "embedded" within a web page, or run on your computer as a "side bar" and requires data from some online application or web site, but it is not a complete shrink-wrapped software application, then it falls under the Widget category.

Wiki: A web site created by a group or collaboration of users

Social networking is taking the Internet by storm. These new social tools can connect people quickly, provide an opportunity for unplanned conversations, and are extremely scalable.

In one example, I found a blog posting by Ross Clennett on ERE.net. He explains how Neal Schon found the new lead vocalist for the band Journey. Below is a condensed version of Ross's blog.[12] This story is relevant to our Attract, Retain, and Repel approach. YouTube allows for video content to be uploaded and viewed by anyone. I have seen people post a "talking resume" on YouTube and send that to recruiters or directly to hiring managers. It is a way for both the job seeker and the recruiting team to see a live demonstration of a skill set.

The story revolves around the rock band Journey, which has existed in various guises since 1973. In 2008 Journey founder and lead guitarist Neal Schon was attempting to recruit a new lead vocalist to replace the departed Perry. Frustrated with the options he had auditioned live, Schon turned to the Internet and spent hours surfing scores of YouTube videos, looking at bands and singers to see whether he might discover what he was looking for online.

Amongst the many wannabes and try-hards, he stumbled upon a video by a popular Filipino cover band, The Zoo.

Schon listened in amazement as 40-year-old lead singer Arnel Pineda belted out a stunning and note-perfect version of one of Journey's biggest 1980s hits, "Faithfully" (amongst many other cover versions The Zoo had posted on YouTube).

Schon messaged The Zoo via YouTube, and although Pineda initially thought it was a hoax, Schon eventually convinced Pineda he was for real, and asked Pineda whether he was interested in auditioning for the vacant lead singer's role.

Six weeks later, a still shell-shocked Pineda was winging his way to San Francisco for a two-day audition with Journey.

In December 2007, Pineda was announced as Journey's new lead singer, followed three months later by his debut, fronting the band live at a Chilean music festival to an ecstatic fan reaction, glowing reviews, and a television audience of 25 million.

What a fantastic story for the new world of recruitment: a story covering globalization, Web 2.0, and nontraditional sourcing strategies.

What I most love about this tale is that a U.S. rock band, whose fan base is solidly in the Midwest, resisted the temptation to go for a singer who "looked right" and instead recruited the best-performed, most-competent singer, even though he was from Manila, speaks heavily accented English, and doesn't look like Steve Perry (save the long dark hair) or the band's fan demographic.

It would be easy to dismiss this story as unique to music and not relevant to recruiters.

I believe that would be a mistake. Consider that in this Journey-finds-new-lead-singer story, the following occurred via the Internet:

- The employer sourced a potential employee, living in another country, online.
- The employer contacted the potential employee.
- The competence of the potential employee was able to be assessed sufficiently well to arrange a live interview (audition) in another country without any need for a resume.

No recruiter was involved in the process. When you consider the growth of career portals and the rise of online testing of skills, competencies, and motivations, recruitment in the 21st century has only just begun. As we rapidly head towards the 21st century's second decade, are you ready for what's ahead?[13]

This is a great example that clearly indicates that there are new ways to source using social networking sites. But what does it mean for our employment brand? Social networking is the act of socializing in a virtual community, which often takes place between individuals with common interests on an actual technology platform.

The challenges that social networking brings to our organizational culture and, ultimately, to the creation of that authentic and congruent employment brand, involve ownership.

- Who will own the internal social networks? Is this an HR function?
- Is it the IT/IS departments' responsibility to monitor, track, and keep them functioning?
- Who will own the blogs that many of these Generation Y employees set up externally or the ones that are company condoned internally?
- There is legal debate on what can and cannot be posted to these blogs. But, is it an IT/IS responsibility to track and monitor? Or is it an HR duty to "protect the company" from conflict of interest, divulgence of corporate trade secrets, libel, or negative press?

Maybe it's the responsibility of PR (assuming there is a formal PR group). After all, it is all "public" information, and all roads lead back to employment branding.

Whether or not you condone blogs, they are going to continue to exist in increasing numbers. These trends are meaningful. We are headed for more and more digital information. If employees are going to reflect a negative corporate image in the blogs or social networks, then you have deeper issues than whether you should allow them or not. You may have some systemic cultural issues that would shift that consciousness — and these issues need to be addressed. But, we also know you can't please all of the people all of the time, so expect a few disgruntled comments here and learn from them. But if you anticipate that the majority of comments will be a negative reflection of your EVP — the employee experience — then fix that cultural disconnect.

If you're prepared to look at the creation of a blog, ask yourself:

- Are we going to allow an internal blog network?
- Who will monitor it to redflag signs of harassment, discrimination, inappropriate content, or disclosure? What policies need to be established first?
- What are the necessary resources? How many resources is that going to take? Can we do a cost-benefit analysis to figure out if it is worth it?
- If we don't allow the blog, will someone set it up outside the company? If they do, what will our response be? Are there free speech issues to consider?
- What is the strategic value?
- What are the technological considerations?

The last thing you want to see on an employee's desk is a copy of what is possibly destined to be a big seller: *My Job Sucks & I Can't Take It Anymore! Help!*[14]

No matter what kind of brand you build, and no matter how aligned it is to your organizational culture, if it is not authentic and congruent, you can guarantee employees will feel it and, more importantly, spread the word.

The Brand Scan

There is an abbreviated version of the employment branding assessment process. We call this The Brand Scan. If you don't have time to give consideration to all that has been put forth in this chapter, there are six steps[15] to take that can get you significant data quickly:

1. Values assessment and alignment exercise
2. Employee engagement or satisfaction survey data review
3. Job board and job description review
4. Web site evaluation
5. Google investigation of public image — respond vs. react
6. Social network search and evaluation

Afterword

This is where we are going to talk about clarity of thought, the manifestation of thoughts and vibration, and, yes, quantum physics. Why, you ask. Well, it relates to cultural fit, employment branding, and employee engagement. Millions of people are starting to show a deep interest in this thought process. Not only do they "get it," they are starting to look for it in their work experience. This approach may become the next "servant leadership" or "spirit in the workplace" model. We know that we live in an ever-changing world and that there will be more and more schools of thought on how our lives can be healthier and happier.

How tapped into the thought process you may become, and how much your organization will embrace it, will remain to be seen, but I would like you to be aware of it as it relates to how we can Attract, Retain, and Repel employees.

Sherry Anshara is the founder of The QuantumPathic® Center of Consciousness,[1] radio show host, and the author of *Age of Inheritance*.[2] Sherry is also a former high-level sales leader in a *Fortune* 500 company. One day we were talking about how this movement can be integrated into Corporate America, and this is what we came up with around the law of attraction:

> Consciousness is comprised of all of the belief systems of an individual, or, in this case, a group. This composite of belief systems is the foundation from which everything is created — the focus, energy, and activity of an organization is filtered through its consciousness.

So, if the organization has carefully evaluated its belief systems and ensured that employees believe in the same principles, values, or can operate powerfully as a team, it can focus its energy and activity in powerful ways to achieve organizational goals.

If this is not the case, the flow of energy is interrupted. Blocks, in the form of belief system or individuals with incongruent belief systems, hinder the forward momentum of the corporation.

In terms of consciousness, CULTURE means THE CULT YOU ARE. A cult is a group that embraces the same belief systems. There is a deep level of connection, and members of the group act together for their beliefs or cause. This unified direction and focus is a powerful force.

The first step is knowing clearly and consciously what you are as an organization. This must be articulated in clear, consistent terms. You must live your values. People know if you mean it — their instincts and intuition tell them instantly if you mean what you say, and your actions show it.

If your organization has defined its values and lives them every day, in every decision it makes and action it takes, you (the company) create a vibration appropriate to what you stand for. Your employees will feel it, and so will your vendors and your customers. It is a way of being that resonates clearly and will attract those who are a fit for that vibration.

If your organization is unclear about its values, or not living them, this incongruence will also resonate. Whether they know exactly what the issue is or not, they will feel that something is off. This will cause confusion as people try to figure out the truth and where they stand.

By being your ideal culture, you will attract the right people and clearly feel when someone is not a fit. The contrast will be easy to identify. And it will begin to snowball as you add to the energy one employee at a time.

The consciousness of the world is shifting. This shift has created an opening in the corporate world for feeling and being. Individuals no longer wish to compartmentalize their lives, to separate themselves from how they contribute at work. The desire is to bring your whole being to the organization and to contribute and grow yourself and your company together. This desire brings a whole new level of meaning to work: It's no longer about a job — it's about a position. It's not about fitting into a job description — it's about creating and expanding yourself and the company.

It's all about that journey to find the best *fit*. In our lives, we often move in and out consciousness, sometimes figuratively and sometimes quite literally.

Employment Branding Study Results (2006 and 2008)

Does understanding your organizational culture help create an authentic and congruent employment brand that will increase the ROI of recruitment and retention? That was my exact question back in 2006. While speaking at the Illinois State SHRM Conference, I met Chloe Rada from Rada Advertising, a full-service recruitment communications agency headquartered in Chicago. We decided to explore this question. We found that we had the same desire to support organizations in discovering what (or "who," but companies aren't people) they really are and transforming that realization into a strength they can effectively use in all employee interactions, including recruitment and retention activities. This shared belief led to the first collaborative study on organizational culture and employment brand, conducted with our friends at Rada Advertising in November 2006. In the fall of 2008, EMERGE International conducted a follow-up benchmarking study with Kennedy Information, a leading source of research, news, and information for professionals. The quantitative results from both studies will be covered in this Appendix.

Our hypothesis was that companies with an understanding of their true culture would be able to build an authentic and congruent employment brand. Our fundamental philosophy about employment branding going into the study was that it's all about culture. It is vital for a company to understand its organizational culture, to really know what (who, if you prefer) they *are* and what they *are not* so that they can build an authentic and congruent employment brand — a brand that is consistent and believable. Such a brand would attract and retain the *right* employees and repel the ones that just won't fit, which, in turn, would increase the ROI of their recruitment and retention efforts.

Rather than focus on the technology details, we decided to focus on the human system approach to this study. We felt we could run an entire Best Practice study on the technology being deployed in recruitment and retention, but we decided to leave that for another day. This study does not cover ATS, SEO, or SEM programs or processes. We do not dive deep into how recruiters are recruiting or what software or hardware is the best. We briefly cover these recruiting techniques and provide data on where recruiters are recruiting, but more importantly for the purpose of this study, how they may be leveraging these trends to enhance their employment branding efforts.

We looked deeper than just asking if employers had an EVP. We asked if they are creating them and blending them into their employment branding efforts. This is a trend we haven't seen much information on. We also wanted to do research on companies that are "going green." We wanted to test our assumptions around this and find out if there are organizations that actively engage in green recruiting.

Study Parameters

In 2006, 78 companies submitted complete responses and demographic information. In our 2008 study, 241 companies submitted complete responses and demographic information. All individual responses remained anonymous to the companies that responded.

Our study used a three-point Likert scale: agree, neutral, disagree. The quantitative statements were broken into the following dimensions:

1. Competitive edge in recruitment and retention efforts.
2. Responsibility — Who owns employment branding?
3. How employment branding relates to, or integrates with, organizational culture.
4. Resources spent on employment branding efforts.

We also asked five qualitative questions that looked at the challenges and opportunities of employment branding programs, the metrics organizations are using to measure the success of their programs, and how employers are currently marketing their employment brand.

Many of the answers we received in the qualitative section of the survey support the numbers gathered from the quantitative section. We were able to capture supportive themes in each of these response areas.

Study Demographics

From both studies, about two-thirds of the participating organizations state that the HR department is centralized and the remaining one-third of the companies say that Human Resources is decentralized.

Positions held in the organization varied quite a bit and correlate to the size and number of employees within the organization (see Figures A.1 and A.2).

Human Resources, as well as marketing and communications professionals, were invited to participate. In the 2008 study, we asked respondents to specify whether they were an HR recruiter or a contract recruiter.

The company scope also varied, but stayed fairly even relative to the two studies (see Figure A.3). Well over two-thirds of the respondents from both studies are from companies with a national or international scope.

Figure A.1. 2006 Results - Position

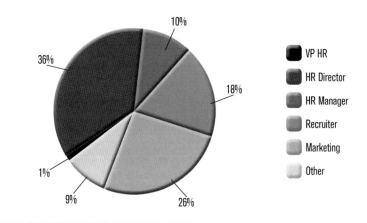

Figure A.2. 2008 Results - Position

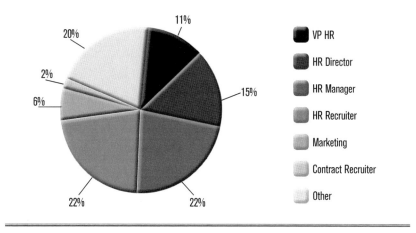

Figure A.3. Number of Employees

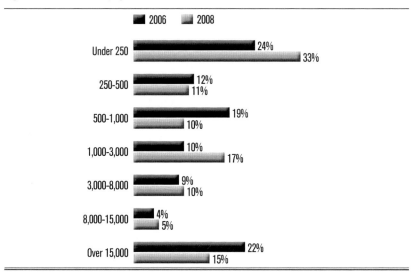

The range of employees is across the board. However, many of the companies share quite a few of the same challenges and opportunities in their recruitment and retention efforts.

Also, in reviewing Figure A.4, budgets range from less than $50,000 to more than $1 million. The majority of respondents said that their recruitment budgets were less than $50,000 (see Figure A.5).

Figure A.4. Company Scope

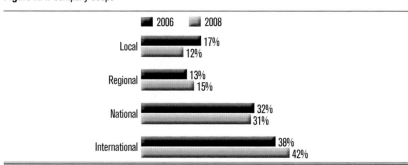

Figure A.5. Recruitment Budgets

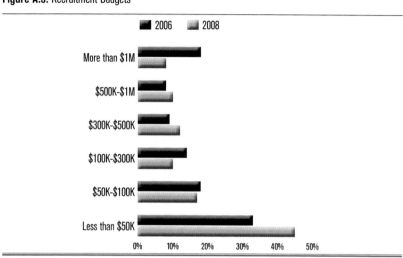

Study Results

Our hypothesis was that companies with an understanding of their true culture would be able to build an authentic and congruent employment brand.

The results show that a company says "employment branding is important to my company and employment branding provides a competitive recruiting edge in our recruiting efforts," yet they do not have branding as one of the top five strategic initiatives for their company in the upcoming year nor do they have budgeted dollars to work on their employment brand in the coming year. This is an indication that while companies say they care, they don't put the action or the money behind the statement.

Professionals know what they need, and they know what works, but getting sponsorship (strategic-level initiative) or senior-level support (budgeted dollars) just falls flat. Professionals are being told to "just do it" but are not being given the tools or resources to "get it done." This is a disservice to the professionals who are championing these efforts without proper funding, resources, and sponsorship.

Let's look at how branding programs are viewed in the context of Attract, Retain, and Repel, and why that may be important to organizations.

Our company's employment brand helps us to attract top talent. Sixty-seven percent of those asked in 2006 agreed, and 60 percent of the 2008 respondents agreed.

My company's employment brand reflects our consumer brand. In 2006, 60 percent of the respondents agreed, yet in 2008 that dropped below half to only 48 percent in agreement.

One of our assumptions was that, since it is a recruitment tool, the responsibility of employment branding would almost exclusively fall to Human Resources. Surprisingly, the results showed that this wasn't the case. In 2006, 51 percent of respondents disagreed with the statement *employment branding at my company is not the responsibility of Human Resources*; in 2008, 50 percent disagreed. The results seem to indicate that employment branding has become more of a joint effort. This shows a positive trend, because, in the past, employment branding efforts were owned by Human Resources and the consumer branding was owned by marketing.

We generally think about "recruitment efforts" in the "attract" phase. HR teams realize that the recruitment efforts are larger than this; something we should look at from start to finish. In this context, it would be starting with a recruitment message; building brand in the context of true organizational culture; having HR programs, processes, and procedures that support your brand; and carrying that through to the exit interview process.

We asked participants to respond to the statement, *by not creating a definitive employment brand we have lost opportunities in our recruitment efforts.* So we can assume this could be at any point in the recruitment process. Fifty-one percent of our 2006 participants agreed and 46 percent of the 2008 respondents agreed. Yet, if we move down stream in the process just a bit, the response to the statement, *our company brand helps us to retain top talent,* 60 percent of the 2006 participants agreed that it did and 56 percent of the 2008 participants agreed. It is interesting to note that the last two responses have a high level of neutrality in both studies with more than 30 percent of the respondents answering neutral. This is an indication that the participants "don't know" or have not measured the branding efforts to determine if they do, in fact, help to attract or retain employees.

The potential exists that metrics are not being deployed in many organizations when it comes to their branding efforts. This point is reinforced by the responses to the statement, *I believe our employees are excited about our employment brand.* Fifty-two percent responded neutral in 2006, and 43 percent responded neutral in 2008. The overwhelming choice of neutral indicates "don't know" or "not sure."

In the qualitative section of the studies, participants were asked, *what metric do you use to measure the effectiveness of your employment branding efforts?* A trend emerged that supports the high level of neutral responses to the statements above. Responses like "metrics, what metrics?" was the norm, which did support the quantitative statements.

Organizational Culture and Branding

We next looked at how building an employment brand fits into the context of an organization's culture.

We saw relatively comparable numbers to the statement, *our company is very clear on what our culture is and is not.* In both studies, more than two-thirds of our participants agreed. In 2006, 56 percent agreed that, the employees understand our company's culture, with a high neutral score of 32 percent. Yet, in 2008, 66 percent agreed and the neutral score dropped to 21 percent. So, if the organization is deploying a quantitative metric, they would better understand if the employees understand the culture or not. We asked if the participants' companies had measured their culture in the past two years — more than 30 percent in both studies said they had not. Less than 50 percent said they had; the other 20 percent were unsure if they had or had not.

With these responses, we notice a slight incongruence with the responses to measuring culture and with being able to better understand brand. Companies know they should measure organizational culture, specifically, because it would help in many of the HR initiatives, but they have not. When asked if an assessment of our company's culture would help uncover our true employment brand, 62 percent agreed, which was higher than the 55 percent in 2006, but still had a high level of neutrality.

Responses to the statement, *by uncovering our true employment brand we could re-align and re-focus our employment branding efforts,* again showed a positive response of 64 percent in 2008 and 69 percent in 2006. When extrapolated to the *Fortune* 1000, this means that well over 300 of the top companies disagree or are neutral.

The most significant response in the organizational culture section was to the statement, *a cultural assessment would allow us to understand the gaps that may exist between what we are and what we desire to be as it relates to retention and recruitment.* An overwhelming 81 percent agreed to that statement in 2006, and 74 percent agreed in 2008. That, we feel, is quite significant. Conducting a cultural assessment allows for the identification of the gaps between what you are and what you want to be, and will give you a specific metric and starting point to build your employment branding program. It sets a baseline and creates a dashboard for ongoing measurement. This will support you in measuring the progress of your employment branding programs as well as the true ROI of your efforts.

This activity has shown that while HR professionals see the value in employment branding, the process or movement has not yet gained senior-level sponsorship (strategic initiative) or organizational legs (dedicated budget dollars) — a trend we would hope to see shift in the coming months and years.

This data also confirms that our fundamental philosophy about employment branding holds true. Branding and culture go hand in hand. Understanding organizational culture is vital to knowing what you are and what you are not in order to build a congruent brand that is consistent and believable.

Qualitative Research: Interviews with Industry Experts

In the search for information on organizational culture and its impact on brand, I reached out to some industry experts for their insights on the topic.

They are individuals who work in the HR space — either providing consulting services to Human Resources or providing information and educational opportunities to HR leaders.

Most of these experts confirm that culture has a direct impact on brand. However, my research indicates that many companies do not set out to create brand in the context of culture, nor do they leverage or measure the effectiveness of that brand.

Debbie McGrath

McGrath is the chief executive officer of HR.com, which helps build great companies by connecting them with the knowledge and resources they need to effectively manage the people side of business. As the global authority, they detail HR best practices to help organizations build great companies through community, collaboration, research, shared best practices, events, and measurements.

Kristen Weirick

Weirick is the director of Talent Acquisition of Global Human Resources at the Whirlpool Corporation. Whirlpool, a leader in the home-appliance industry, has taken a systemic and holistic approach to employment branding. Their considerable efforts are well reflected on their careers site and are to be applauded.

Tom Nightingale

Nightingale is the vice president of Communications and chief marketing officer with Con-way, a leader in the transportation and logistics industry with more than 30,000 employees worldwide. Like Whirlpool, they have also recently transformed their employment-branding initiative.

Louise Kursmark

Kursmark is a principal at Best Impression, one of the leading resume-writing experts in the United States. She is an authority on a wide range of career and employment issues. She has written 18 books about resume writing, interviewing, and executive search strategies.

George Blomgren

Blomgren is recruiting solutions director at The Management Association (MRA). MRA was founded in 1901 and is a not-for-profit employers' organization serving more than 4,000 employers throughout Wisconsin, Illinois, and Iowa.

Todd Raphael

Raphael is the editor in chief for ERE Media. ERE.net has become one of the most respected web sites for information on the recruiting industry. Their trade shows and conferences are ranked among the top for new industry knowledge, and they are well respected for their independent thinking.

Louis Carter

Carter is the president and CEO of Best Practice Institute (BPI). They are a community of leaders dedicated to pioneering and sharing best practices.

Question: On average, do job seekers take into consideration a company's culture before they apply to that organization?

McGrath: Of the majority of hires, the culture of an organization is an afterthought. The majority of the hires are done at an entry- or junior-level. For the more senior positions, more thought is put into the culture and organizational fit of an organization. People in high demand with lots of opportunities will be pickier about organizational fit than those with limited options.

Weirick: Savvy candidates will definitely consider company culture, but it's generally not the first consideration for most candidates — that's usually compensation. However, company culture and a candidate's "fit" into that culture will be one of the primary factors for engagement and retention.

Nightingale: Culture has always been a factor for potential employees when they were considering employment with Con-way. However, it is increasingly becoming a determining factor as Gen Y becomes more a part of our workforce. The level of transparency that they have eliminates any doubt as to the type of culture that they are joining. And, because we believe it's a competitive advantage for us, we are trying to give them the tools they need to know what kind of a culture we deliver as part of our employee value proposition.

Kursmark: Job seekers definitely take culture into consideration — if not on application, then definitely during the interviewing/selection process. Most of the people I work with — top-performing executives with exceptional careers and a load of talent — tell me they're looking for not just "a" job but the right opportunity with the right company, culture, and people. They take this very seriously.

Blomgren: Few job seekers consciously think of things like "culture" or "employer brand," but they are still influenced by these intangibles. For example, they certainly consider an employer's "reputation" (employer brand) with specific attention to "what it's like to work there" (culture). Aside from concrete criteria like salary, benefits, and specific job opportunities, "what it's like to work there" is influential on employment decisions. In years of working with job seekers, I've come to believe that the more sophisticated job seekers weigh company culture even more than immediate job opportunities. The metaphor I often use is that star performers care more about what team they play for than what position they might play initially.

Raphael: When they know someone at their prospective company, they talk to that person. When they don't know someone, they pick up clues from multiples sources — including many sources that employers forget that employers look at. These include:

- The company's web site
- Outside web sites such as Vault.com
- Business and general magazines
- Recruiters who work for the company
- Outside recruiters
- People who work the booths at job fairs
- The candidate's experience during the interview

It comes down to the sense they get of the culture from the communication they receive from the company: Are they formal? Informal? Rushed? Casual? Goofy? Witty? Hip?

Carter: Job seekers do consider a company's culture before applying to work in an organization, dependent upon their economic situation. Potential employees who are serious about a career with an organization will learn as much as possible about the company culture before applying. The intersection of the company culture, strengths of the employee, and the structure of the organization influences employee recruitment and retention.

Question: If culture is a factor in job or company selection, what approach are candidates using to identify or understand the company culture before they apply?

McGrath: Two of the most common approaches are:

First, by asking friends who work there what it's like. And second by trying to judge the fit based on the interview. This is not always a good representation of the organization's fit as interviews are like sales jobs. The recruiter is trying to sell you on the organization and may often not portray the actual culture of the organization properly.

Weirick: Many times they'll rely on the interview experience and their interactions with various employees during that process. Smart candidates may request to meet specifically with other employees "like them" (potential peers and/or diverse employees) to get their take on working in the organization. Additionally, many — especially university candidates — are using social media sites to connect with current company employees and get an understanding of the company culture.

Nightingale: These days, we make it pretty easy for a candidate to find out about our culture because it's a critical element of our employee value proposition. Some of the things that we have done include:

- Creating LinkedIn groups to make it easier for candidates to pose questions of our people.
- Building a YouTube channel where people can see what it's like to work with us, the things that we are most passionate about, and the awards that personify our culture.[1]
- Adding work/life profiles to our web site showing real employees and how to strike the right balance between their life inside Con-way and their life outside Con-way.
- Supporting employees who have the opportunity to get out and speak publicly or blog about the company.

In years past, we took the stance that our values and our culture was not something that we should "market" to an employee. In fact, up until 2007, we did not even make them publicly available on our web site. We now recognize that it creates a competitive advantage for us in the war for talent so we give prospective employees every opportunity to evaluate their fit with our culture and values before they even apply for a job.

I believe people use the basics — the Internet, the company web site, the company blog, other blogs, their LinkedIn network, and their personal network. And, if they're smart, they talk to as many people within the hiring company as possible just to get a sense of who the people are, how they interact and communicate, and how the organization flows and functions.

Kursmark: As mentioned, they may not research it closely before they apply, but during the interview process they are looking up the company online, reading news stories about the company and its executives, and tapping into their network to find out the "real scoop" from current and former employees, customers, and business partners. Nowadays, of course, they can go beyond their immediate network to social networking sites, where they can easily find a connection to most any company. Beyond the initial research, candidates are assessing the quality of the interview process and the behaviors they observe. If they are treated poorly (or see others being treated poorly), left waiting, encounter rude interviewers, are left dangling without communication, and otherwise treated as if they have little value, they form a lasting negative opinion of that company. In a survey I did about 18 months ago, 25 percent of respondents said that something had happened during the interview process that made them decide not to work for a company!

Blomgren: There's the rub. It's widely recognized that it's hard to get a good handle on [a] potential employer's company culture. There simply is no effective, easy approach. [I know a career coach who has come up with some clever ideas, but they really just illustrate how hard you would have to try to get even vague insights into company culture.] Lacking any direct methods to gauge company culture, job seekers rely on word of mouth. If you haven't worked for ABC Company, you probably know someone who has, or know someone who knows someone. Even though we all know that "the grapevine" isn't reliable, whatever message it carries tends to carry a lot of weight. Consider Wal-Mart: no doubt they've spent a lot of money to combat the popular perception that they aren't a good employer, but the grapevine trumps any of their formal "employer branding" efforts.

Carter: Employment candidates are increasingly savvy when identifying what a company can do for them. A certain amount of transparency goes a long way. If everything inside is "top secret," potential employees will still find a way to sniff out the information.

While potential employees utilize ever more connected business networks, it is impossible to have a true picture of company culture until one sets foot in the organization. If there is a strong disconnect between the employment brand and the company culture, potential employees will recognize it quickly.

During the interview, potential employees will evaluate the style of the interview and interviewer, as well as the description of work and responsibility for the position. If possible, the interviewee will try to discern whether the "on paper" description of the job matches the actual deliverables. Job seekers will also take matters into their own hands, asking questions about responsibilities, teamwork, advancement opportunities, and company culture.

Question(s): What are some critical cultural elements that would attract and retain a candidate? And what would repel them in the first place?

McGrath: To attract a candidate, we need:

- Participation and high ranking in programs like the "Best Places to Work"
- Documented success stories available to candidates for their employee portal
- Mention the fact that they do care about culture, actively measure it and take action on nonperformers
- Showcase the culture as part of the employment brand

To keep them employed (retain):

- Measure and take action on people not living the values of the organization.
- Clearly live the values of the organization.
- Clearly state the values and the culture of the organization.
- Ensure managers reward people living the culture.

Weirick: To attract and retain, we need:

- Nature/quality of peers and leadership within the organization
- Company progressiveness/innovativeness
- Level of employee responsibility and accountability
- Level of empowerment for individual employees
- Opportunities for growth/development
- Company reputation/history
- Level of corporate social responsibility

The elements mentioned above will have varying degrees of importance based on the individual candidate. They are also the same things that will repel candidates (in varying degrees) if they are lacking.

Nightingale: Attract — we want people to seek us out who are believers in team-work and who will leverage the collective strengths of our employees by engaging in constructive dialogue and active listening to foster an environment of cooperation and *esprit de corps*. We seek people with unquestionable integrity, ethics, and who will demonstrate respect in all interactions to foster an environment of trust while accepting responsibility and accountability. We attract candidates who demonstrate commitment by persevering to achieve goals through demonstrated reliability and innovative use of resources. And, we want candidates who are drawn to an environment where excellence is the standard but they still strive for continuous improvement.

Retain — retention is all about the consistent delivery of the employment value proposition that you marketed to the potential employee. In Con-way's case, if we have effectively attracted the right candidates and they were truly attracted to and aligned with all elements of our employment value proposition, then we stand a very good chance of retaining them. It's really only when someone thought they were aligned to our employment value proposition and later discovered that they did not buy into the culture that they leave.

Repel — in our case, we hope that any candidate who is considering employment with us aligns with our culture and values. If they look at any element of our employment value proposition and feel that our gears will not mesh with theirs, it's better for everyone if they self-select out. For example, if someone has had a career where they have played on the ethical fringes, we hope that they look at our integrity value and walk away.

Kursmark: Attract a candidate:
- Clear statement of values that align with candidate's values ... and then behavior that matches that statement
- Opportunities to learn, grow, and advance. This is a *critical* factor for employees at all levels!
- Being valued for their expertise
- Being part of a cohesive team
- Being given challenging assignments.
- Having a mentor
- Flexible schedules
- Company having an exciting future and a clear strategy

- Company committing resources to people and technology
- Company having a clear brand and a defined market space (not just "a" company but "the" company for something)
- Having an executive team that can be respected and learned from
- Other cultural factors will vary ... Some want a "family atmosphere;" others might want a face-paced, high-energy culture, etc. Companies need to express true brand/culture so they attract people who want what they have!

Keep them employed (retain):
- All of the above!
- Coming through on promises of new assignments, training programs, advancement, etc.
- Taking seriously — and acting on — the findings of employee surveys (not just collecting the data)
- Opportunities to learn and grow. This should *never* be overlooked, no matter the level of the employee. For a nursing home I was working with, we worked to overcome the stereotype that nursing aides were motivated solely by money and that for an extra 25 cents an hour they would jump ship to work at McDonald's. In reality, what they wanted was to stay in their jobs, learn new things and be able to advance — just a little! — and be looked up to by junior aides as a source of knowledge and experience. It wasn't just about the money — in fact, money was much less important than management thought.
- Clear career paths and serious attention given to advancing employees to the next level

Repel them in the first place
- Culture that is not attractive to them (e.g., "family atmosphere" for the Type A go-getter who wants the go-go atmosphere)
- Discord between what is claimed and what is displayed (e.g., "our employees are our #1 asset!" then seeing employees treated rudely while on-site interviewing; or claim that education and advancement are valued but hearing otherwise from current/past employees)
- Being treated rudely in any way by any employee
- Experiencing arrogant or unprepared interviewers

Not being given even the courtesy of a reply to a job application, e-mail, phone call, or other communication

Blomgren: Different job seekers will resonate with different cultural elements, so it's hard to generalize. But a short list of elements that would appeal to most job seekers includes:

- "ABC takes good care of its people."
- "There's room for growth at ABC."
- "ABC is a successful company, one that offers good job security."
- "ABC offers generous benefits and above-market compensation."

What would repel them in the first place?

- "ABC has really high turnover."
- "ABC doesn't pay its people fairly."
- "The company is in financial trouble."

Raphael: It depends on the candidate, so there's not one answer. Some people want very competitive environments. Others want to work in teams. Some people want to work in a family atmosphere where people play softball after work. Others want their own life outside of work.

To retain them, it's the same as above, with one exception. Candidates expect the culture to match what they've been "sold" in the hiring process. If they're told people at the company have a life, have families, have time for their families, and so on, and then they get there only to find themselves receiving instant messages from their boss at all hours of the day, they're going to be disappointed.

Carter: Attract a candidate — attracting and retaining a candidate go hand in hand. A company that attracts many candidates, but few that are either qualified or a good fit for the company, will lose money in the long run. It is important that a company fully understands its mission, values, and needs. Additionally, the company must communicate these needs to potential job candidates, and interview candidates who will fill those needs.

Retain employees — The number-one key to keeping talented employees with the company is a good, symbiotic match between employer and employee. Both parties must deliver what is promised during the interview. The employer must live the employment brand or culture in day-to-day operations. The employee must represent the picture he or she presented during the interview. Failure to do so will create friction between the employer and the employee, leading to either termination (by the employer) or departure (by the employee). Deliver what they expect when they are interviewed. If you have an employment brand, be sure that it carries through your entire daily culture.

For example: The interviewers present a company's culture as a laid-back atmosphere with open doors and little structure, with everyone coming and going freely. During the first day on the job and a new employee sees, that, rather than the laid back atmosphere expected, everyone is tense and yelling about the bottom line. In this case, the company did not accurately represent the brand.

Another example: A self-proclaimed vegetarian working at an eco-friendly company with a vegan cafeteria goes out after work with some co-workers on a Friday night and orders steak. Not-so-mock horror ensues as his co-workers put down their forks and exchange "looks." Perhaps not the end of the world, but the employee [misrepresented] himself at the interview, in a way that was related to the job.

Employee retention will take care of itself if the following conditions are met: both parties accurately present during the interview process, and both parties carry through their own "brand" or identification during employment. In a truly functional company, what is good for the company is good for the employee, and vice versa. This balance will keep the company functional and profitable, and the employees content and contributing.

Repel them from applying in the first place: Well, I would not recommend communicating the following employment brand publically, even if this is your brand: "At Company X, we over-promise and under-deliver. We tell you that you will be involved in exciting projects, but really we just need some more secretaries with fancy titles." Another no-go would be: "We'll tell you that it is OK that you can't write, spell, or groom yourself, hire you anyway and then end up firing you because you aren't a 'good fit.'"

Depending upon how complicated the application process is, the potential employee is unlikely to apply if it is apparent that he or she will not be a good fit for the company. The reputation, or brand of the company, if it is well-communicated or well-known, can encourage or discourage potential job candidates, depending upon their skills and interest.

Question: Does the average job seeker look for an employment brand when applying to an organization, and, if so, why?

McGrath: Very few companies have an awesome employment brand. What makes a difference here is that if an applicant has a choice they will always apply to the place with a good employment brand over the one without a known employment brand. Case in point, if you want to work in the airline industry and live in Dallas, you would hope to work for Southwest over American Airlines. If you live in California and you want to work in the high-tech industry, you would pick Google over Yahoo!, but you may pick Yahoo! over Oracle.

Nightingale: Yes, they definitely look for it. While they may not be cognizant of it, they are using the employment brand as shorthand for the employment value proposition. And the employment value proposition is how they meter their risk. Prospective employees make decisions just like any buyer. They innately evaluate jobs on the same three risk dimensions that Dr. Raymond Corey at Harvard published in the late 1960s. The employment brand becomes their gauge for:

- Performance risk. Will the company give me the tools I need to do my job and will my job actually contribute to the goals of the organization?
- Price risk. Will the company pay me a fair wage for the work I do and my contribution to the goals of the organization?
- Psychosocial risk. Will I look good or bad for choosing this employer?

Kursmark: I'm not sure the average job seeker knows what to look for (or perhaps even what an employment brand is!). But job seekers do look for clues as to what it's like to work there, what kind of culture the web site, job postings, and interactions reveal; and so forth. So if a company made the effort to express its employment brand at every point possible, candidates *would* notice.

You have only to read the blog on *Fortune*'s "Best Companies to Work For" to see that the employment experience is not the same for all employees at one company. This drives home the importance of clarifying the employment brand and making "living the brand" a strategic priority right from the top ... identifying and rewarding the right behaviors. Also, hiring the right people! My guess is that a lot of the disgruntled bloggers were the wrong fit for the job or the company in the first place.

Blomgren: Again, to the average job seeker, employment brand equals "reputation." Job seekers don't much care that an employer has spent a lot of time, money or energy promoting its employer brand. All they care about is the nature of that brand.

I have two additional thoughts. One, some employers believe that their employer brand is the sum total of whatever they have tried to promote as their employer brand: the slogan, the billboard, the employee referral program they rolled out. What they fail to realize is that employer branding is happening regardless of their efforts. Especially through word of mouth. Formal employer branding is most effective when it is consistent with the company's reputation. In other words, when it is consistent with the true company culture.

Furthermore, building on the idea that word of mouth is the most powerful and ubiquitous channel for employer branding, keep in mind that the most powerful and "viral" component isn't statements like "ABC takes good care of its people."

Rather, it takes the form of stories. Stories that illustrate how ABC does (or doesn't) take good care of its people. Such as "my friend Joe knows this disabled guy who worked at ABC. He wanted to participate in the Special Olympics. ABC not only gave him comp time for the event itself, they also gave him comp time for training!" Stories (true or not) take on a life of their own, and are tremendously powerful. I've always been intrigued by the idea that a company can start its own mythology, it's own "bank" of stories, the kind of stories that happy employees would want to share with friends and acquaintances.

Raphael: They may not use that terminology, but they are attracted to employers like Google, Patagonia, Herman Miller, Ikea, Trader Joe's, Southwest Airlines, and others that are perceived to have distinct and interesting cultures.

Carter: Job seekers will pay attention to an employment brand, and may gravitate toward a specific type of culture or "brand." What potential employees will look for, more than anything else, is the connection between the brand and the execution of the brand. An employment brand means nothing if it is not carried through in the day-to-day culture of the company.

Culture and brand are two of several components that affect best practice recruitment and retention. Perhaps most importantly, we need to consider the competence of an employee. When organizations pre-qualify employee competence in specific job functions, they reduce the risk of employee failure on-the-job and thus improve employee retention. I believe position-specific job competencies that are qualified by verified rating sources is integral to the success of an organization's talent strategy.

I like to think of organizations as systems, much as a family system. The way employers and employees relate is both a social and a business interaction. For either families or organizations to function well, all parties involved must contribute appropriately. Information flow and benefits cannot go in only one direction. Too often, the case is that employers cater entirely to the employees. It is well and good for employees to be happy; however, they need to be happy *and* productive. This is best accomplished when an organization knows exactly what it needs employees to do and structures itself to allow employees to contribute in a meaningful and cost-effective way. When an employee's contributions are valued and they can tell that, they will be happy and productive, and will stick around.

Additionally, as discussed above, it is imperative that a company understands itself, its brand, its needs, and its goals — and aggressively markets and communicates those to future clients, customers and employees. Then, the company needs to live the brand, or the goals. If the outward face of a company is 180 degrees different than the inside culture, clients and employees will see right through it and, at that point, a company becomes dysfunctional. A company unable to produce products or provide services due to organizational breakdown and high employee turnover will have done itself a disservice by misrepresenting itself. Again, the key to maintaining a highly functioning atmosphere is balance of inputs and regulations between employers and employees.

Successful companies implement best practices in terms of employment branding, recruitment, retention, and management. From the beginning, the company and the employee lay the groundwork for successful relationships. Each side expects the best from the other: respect, understanding, professionalism, and clear expectations are the cornerstones of a successful employer-employee relationship.

Concluding Thoughts on the Interviews

Most people do not understand branding. Even the majority of those firms committed to building an employment brand still have a hard time measuring it, and, more important, living it. Debbie McGrath has seen a lot of brands, and it was interesting to me the company names she chose, as well as all the participants. It gave me confirmation that I had chosen good examples for the body of this book. I think we all know a good brand when we see one.

Kristen Weirick and Tom Nightingale gave excellent corporate examples in their answers. The higher the level within the organization someone is, the more strategic they tend to think. That is to be expected. High-level officers in global companies will expect a higher level of sophistication, education, and business savvy from the candidate pool. If a high-level candidate is not interested in learning about the culture, then that should send up a red flag. It may be an indication of whether they plan to stick around or not. It might also be an indication that they are not "clued in" enough on the people side of the business — the culture. Being clued in and questioning culture will be even more prominent if the economy continues to see more and more consolidation, which has a profound impact on cultural transformation and cultural integration.

Louise Kursmark brings up some excellent points, and they all have to do with the "experience." The approach to getting hired has evolved over the last half-dozen years with the changes in technology but there is one step in the final decision-making process for both the candidate and the employer: the human interaction during an interview process. This snap shot in time often is the critical moment of truth, for both parties. As a former director of Human Resources, I have conducted hundreds of interviews, and each interview has been a new experience. Everyone is different, so if we think we can ask the same set of questions and pull the same answer sets and base the hiring decision on these answers, we can easily miss some of the best candidates out there.

George Blomgren's perspective about "story" is one to really examine. In 1999, when I was doing research for my first book,[2] I dove deep into what organizational culture really is, how it's formed, who owns it, who shapes it, who creates it, and who maintains it. It was fascinating to find companies like the Mayo Clinic that have actually hired cultural anthropologists to discover how the culture was formed. It's about the assumptions and stories. Assumptions are formed by the employee experience, which is their day-to-day interaction with the people within the culture. From this interaction they observe, much like a researcher, even though they are doing this passively vs. actively. From those assumptions they create the stories, and those stories are told over and over again until they become lore, or, in some cases, urban legend.

Todd Rapheal brings up a key point that matches with the whole cultural-fit approach. He makes the point that candidates expect the culture to match what they are told, or sold. So the point about ensuring an employment brand is created in the context of true organizational culture, one that it is authentic and congruent, is correct. If a candidate is sold one thing and experiences something else, be prepared for turnover — it's almost guaranteed.

Louis Carter made some excellent points: comparing the organizational system to a family unit; everyone has to contribute for it to be functional. The flip side, from a branding point of view, is that if the brand does not match the culture, it sets itself up for dysfunction, and that resides in all three phases of Attract, Retain, and Repel.

Additional SHRM-Published Books

The EQ Interview: Finding Employees with High Emotional Intelligence
By Adele B. Lynn

The Essentials of Corporate Communications & Public Relations
By Wendy Bliss

Hiring Success: The Art and Science of Staffing Assessment and Employee Selection
By Steven Hunt

HR and the New Hispanic Workforce: A Comprehensive Guide to Cultivating and Leveraging Employee Success
By Louis E.V. Nevaer and Vaso Perimenis Ekstein

HR Competencies: Mastery at the Intersection of People and Business
By Dave Ulrich, Wayne Brockbank, Dani Johnson, Kurt Sandholtz, and Jon Younger

Igniting Gen B & Gen V: The Rules of Engagement for Boomers, Veterans, and Other Long-Terms on the Job
By Nancy S. Ahlrichs

Investing in People: Financial Impact of Human Resource Initiatives
By Wayne Cascio and John Boudreau

Never Get Lost Again: Navigating Your HR Career
By Nancy E. Glube and Phyllis G. Hartman

Reinventing Talent Management: How to Maximize Performance in the New Marketplace
By William Schiemann

Strategic Staffing: A Comprehensive System for Effective Workforce Planning, 2nd edition
By Thomas P. Bechet

For additional books, see www.shrm.org/publications/books/pages/default.aspx.

Endnotes

Chapter 1

1. The seven books in the series are, in order *The Gunslinger* (New York: Viking, 2003); *The Drawing of the Three* (New York: Viking Adult, 2003); *The Waste Lands* (New York: Viking Adult, 2003); *Wizard and Glass* (New York: Viking Adult, 2003); *Wolves of the Calla* (New York: Donald M. Grant/Scribner, 2003); *Song of Susannah* (New York: Donald M. Grant/Scribner, 2004); and *The Dark Tower* (New York: Donald M. Grant/Scribner, 2004).

2. Jim Collins and Jerry I. Porras, *Built to Last: Successful Habits of Visionary Companies* (New York: Collins Business, 2004).

3. Jim Collins, *Good to Great: Why Some Companies Make the Leap ... and Others Don't* (New York: Collins Business, 2001).

4. O'Connell, Matthew and Mei-Chuan Kung, "The Cost of Employee Turnover," *Industrial Management*. ProQuest. January-February 2007, pp. 14ff. Quoted in Carol Morrison, "Retention before the Fact," *Performance and Profits*, April 2007, vol. 2, no. 4. Available at: http://www.amanet.org /performance-profits/editorial.cfm?Ed=498.

Chapter 2

1. EMERGE International, Cultural Due Diligence Readiness Assessment, 2000.

2. Collins and Porras, 2004.

3. See http://www.marines.com/main/index/making_marines/culture /traditions/semper_fidelis.

4. Anne Lee, "How to Build a Lasting Brand," *Fast Company*, Sept. 2, 2008.

5. Annie Brooking, *Intellectual Capital: Core Assets for the Third Millennium* (London and New York: International Thomson Business Press, 1996).

Chapter 3

1. Robert Rodriguez, "Creating an Employment Brand for Your Organization," *Talent Management Magazine*, November 2006.
2. Ruhal Dooley, Deb Levine, and Audra Russell, "Branding Trends and Communicable Diseases," *HR Magazine*, December 2007.
3. See http://www.marketingpower.com/_layouts/Dictionary.aspx?dLetter=B.
4. See http://www.nasrecruitment.com/.
5. Employment Branding white paper, "Marketing Your Company as the Place to Work," November 2007, Careerbuilder.com.
6. ERE.net, "Employment Branding: The only long-term recruiting solution," Dr. John Sullivan, January 7, 2008.
7. This commercial is available for total access viewing at http://www.responsibilityproject.com/about/.
8. Mark Murphy and Andrea Burgio-Murphy, *The Deadly Sins of Employee Retention* (Charleston, SC: BookSurge, 2006).
9. See http://www.mcmurry.com/about_us/culture.php.
10. 2008 Employment branding study, EMERGE International and Kennedy Information.

Chapter 4

1. See Dan Fletcher, "A Brief History of the Tylenol Poisonings," *Time*, February 9, 2009. Accessible at http://www.time.com/time/nation/article/0,8599,1878063,00.html.
2. Bianna Golodryga, "Pink Slip E-Mail Error," ABC News, September 4, 2008. Accessible at: http://blogs.abcnews.com/moneybeat/2008/09/pink-slip-e-mai.html.
3. www.jwtintelligence.com. Work in progress, 10 Trends for 2009.

Chapter 5

1. Accessible at: http://www.antarctic-circle.org/advert.htm.
2. Towers Perrin, "Global Workforce Study," June 2007. Accessible at: http://www.towersperrin.com/tp/showhtml.jsp?url=global/publications/gws/index.htm&country=global.
3. Manpower and Mike Desmarais, "Let Your Call Center Customer Service Representatives be a Judge," September, 2006. Accessible at: http://www.manpower.com/research/research.cfm?chooseyear=2006&categoryid=2.

4.   Robert J. Vance, "Effective Practice Guidelines—Employee Engagement and Commitment," SHRM Foundation, 2006. Accessible at: http://www.shrm .org/searchcenter/Pages/Results.aspx?k=Molson%20Coors.

5.   John Thackray, "Feedback for Real," *Gallup Management Journal*. Accessible at: http://www.artsusa.org/pdf/events/2005/conv/gallup_q12.pdf.

6.   BlessingWhite, "The State of Employee Engagement 2008," April 2008. Accessible at: http://www.blessingwhite.com/Research.asp?pid=1.

7.   Press Ganey, "Employee and Nurse Check-Up Report," Press Ganey Associates, Inc., October 2008. Accessible at: http://www.pressganey.com/galleries /default-file/Employee_Nurse_Check-Up_10-08-08.pdf.

8.   Alanah May Eriksen, quoting Paul Hortop, "Quarter of workers' time online is personal," *nzherald.co.nz*, September 2008. Accessible at: http://www. nzherald.co.nz/technology/news/article.cfm?c_id=5&objectid=10534055.

9.   See Lisa Guerin, *Smart Policies for Workplace Technologies: Email, Blogs, Cell Phones & More* (Berkeley, CA: Nolo/SHRM, 2009).

10. Todd Nordstrom quoting Drs. Kevin and Jackie Freiberg, "Boom! A Wake Up Call for Life at Work," *Go Jobing*, Fall 2007.

11. Lizz Pellet and P.J. Bouchard, *Getting Your Shift Together: Making Sense of Organizational Culture and Change, Introducing Cultural Due Diligence,* (Cave Cree, AZ:CCI Press, 2000).

12. *USA Today*, Tuesday, September 4, 2007. 3B.

13. *USA Today*, Wednesday, May 21, 2008. 3B.

14. Wikipedia.org. Accessible at: http://en.wikipedia.org/wiki/Chick-fil-A.

15. Accessible at: http://www.chick-fil-a.com/#faqs.

16. Libby Sartain and Martha I. Finney, *HR from the Heart: Inspiring Stories and Strategies for Building the People Side of Great Business* (New York: AMACOM, 2003).

Chapter 6

1.   E. Ted Prince, "The Valuation Approach to ROI," *Chief Learning Officer* (October 2006). Available at: http://www.clomedia.com/features/2006 /October/1567/index.php.

2.   Mike Nale, "Even in a Recession, Employment Branding is Worth the Risk," ERE.net, Jun 18, 2008. Accessible at: http://www.ere.net/2008/06/18/ even-in-a-recession-employment-branding-is-worth-the-risk/.

3.   Douglas B. Holt, *How Brands Become Icons: The Principles of Cultural Branding* (Boston: Harvard Business School Publishing, 2004).

4.   Thomas N. Robinson et al, "Effects of Fast Food Branding on Young Children's Taste Preferences," *Archives of Pediatrics & Adolescent Medicine*, 161:792-797, August 2007. Accessible at: http://archpedi.ama-assn.org /cgi/content/abstract/161/8/792.

5.   Peter Weddle, "How e-Brands Work and Don't Work," April 2005. Accessible at: http://www.weddles.com/recruiternews/issue.cfm?Newsletter=157.

6.   Carol Morrison, "Retention Before the Fact," Institute for Corporate Productivity, April 2007. Accessible at: http://www.amanet.org/performance-profits/editorial.cfm?Ed=498.

7.   RetirementJobs.com, "Flexibility Ranks First, Entrepreneurship Last, When Baby Boomers and Active Retirees Seek Retirement Jobs," June 2006. Accessible at: http://www.retirementjobs.com/aboutus/press/06_21_2006.html.

Chapter 7

1.   See "History of Federal Minimum Wage Rates Under the Fair Labor Standards Act, 1938-2007," U.S. Department of Labor, Employment Standards Administration. Accessible at: www.dol.gov/ESA/minwage/chart.htm.

2.   See generally U.S. Census Bureau data at: "Current Population Reports: Consumer Income Reports from 1946-2007," located at www.census.gov /prod.

3.   American Hospital Association and The First Consulting Group, "When I'm 64: How Boomers Will Change Health Care," May 2007. Accessible at: www.aha.org/aha/content/2007/pdf/070508-boomerreport.pdf.

4.   Ibid.

5.   AARP, "Best Employers 2007." Accessible at: http://www.aarp.org/money /work/articles/best_employers_2007.html.

6.   American Society on Aging, "2007 Business and Aging Awards." Accessible at: http://www.asaging.org/asav2/awards/business_2007.cfm?submenu1 =business.

7.   AARP, "Best Employers for Workers over 50." Accessible at: http://www. aarp.org/aarp/presscenter/pressrelease/articles/2006_list_best_employers .html.

8.   Ken Dychtwald et al, *Workforce Crisis: How to Beat the Coming Shortage of Skills And Talent* (Boston: Harvard Business School Press, 2006).

9.   Jim Haudan and Rich Berens, "High-Tech Learning for Low-Tech Employees," *Chief Learning Officer Magazine*, May 2007. Available at: www.clomedia.com /features/2007/May/1833/index.php. Quoting from Lee Rainie, "Digital

'Natives' Invade the Workplace," Pew Internet & American Life Project, September 27, 2006.

10. Sharon Birkman Fink, "Doing What Comes Naturally," Kennedy Information's Recruiting Trends On-line publication, December 2008. Available at: http://www.recruitingtrends.com/issues/44_12/thoughtleadership/1256-1.html.

11. JWT, Work in Progress: 10 Trends for 2007 (December 2006). Available at: http://www.jwtintelligence.com/.

12. Next Step, "Workforce of the Future," 2008. Accessible at: http://www.nextstepgrowth.com/workshops/wf_multi_gen.php#.

Chapter 8

1. "Using Your Firm's Environmentally Friendly Practices in Recruiting," ERE.net, June 4, 2007.

2. Timberland corporate web site at: http://www.timberland.com/corp/index.jsp?clickid=topnav_corp_txt, March 2009.

3. Whole Foods web site, http://www.wholefoodsmarket.com/values/corevalues.php, March 2009.

4. See http://www.wholefoodsmarket.com/company/index.php.

5. Ibid.

6. See http://www.ti.com/corp/docs/csr/index.shtml?DCMP=TIFooterTracking&HQS=Other+OT+footer_csr 2009.

7. Tara Weiss, "Bain Grows 'Green Team' Concept," Forbes.com, June 6, 2007. Accessible at: http://www.forbes.com/2007/06/06/environment-ban-green-lead-citizen-cx_tw_0606green.html.

8. Alison Martin, "Lights of for Earth Hour," Workopolis.com, March 28, 2008.

9. *USA Today*, November 14, 2008.

10. Tandberg, "Corporate Environmental Behavior and the Impact on Brand Values," October 2007. Available at: http://www.ivci.com/pdf/corporate-environmental-behaviour-and-the-impact-on-brand-values.pdf.

11. Stanford Graduate School Study, 2007. The video file is available at: http://www.gsb.stanford.edu/news/research/corporate_social_responsibility.shtml.

12. Anne Moore Odell, "How Companies' Climate Plans Affect Financial Performance," GreenBiz.com, November 6, 2007. Available at: http://www.greenbiz.com/feature/2007/11/06/how-companies-climate-plans-affect-financial-performance.

13. LEED is created by the U.S. Green Building Council and is accessible at: www.gbc.com.

14. http://www.design21sdn.com/organizations/254.

15. Available at: http://www.youtube.com/watch?v=VSNFE6eUjfY&feature =related.

16. Dawn Dzurilla, "Renewable Energy Firms Strike Gold with Green Employee Benefits," *Climate Biz*, January 14, 2008. Available at: http://www.climate-biz.com/blog/2008/01/14/renewable-energy-firms-strike-gold-with-green-employee-benefits.

Chapter 9

1. Chuck Salter, "Tivoli Systems Inc.: Showing Its True Color," *Fast Company*, March 2000. Accessible at: http://www.fastcompany.com/magazine/33 /updates.html.

2. Sue Cartwright and Gary L. Cooper, *Managing Mergers, Acquisitions & Strategic Alliances: Integrating People and Cultures*, 2d edition (Oxford and Boston: Butterworth-Heinemann, 1996).

3. Thomas J. Peters and Robert H. Waterman Jr., *In Search of Excellence: Lessons from America's Best-Run Companies* (New York: HarperCollins, 1982).

4. Rodney D. Fralicx and C.J. Bolster, "Preventing Culture Shock," *Modern Healthcare*, vol. 11, August 1997.

5. Edgar H. Schein, *Organizational Culture and Leadership* (San Francisco: Jossey-Bass, 2004).

Chapter 10

1. ERE.net, "Don't be fooled by what employment branding is – Part 2," February 5, 2007.

2. Patrick J. Kiger, "Talent Acquisition Special Report: Burnishing the Brand," *Workforce Management*, October 2007. Available at: http://www.fia-us.org /news_events/RecommendedReading/Talent%20Acquisition%20Special %20Report%20--%20Brunishing%20the%20Brand.pdf.

3. http://www.thephantomwriters.com/video-article-marketing.html.

4. Lindsay Edmonds Wickman, "A New Kind of Work Environment for a New Kind of Generation," *Chief Learning Officer*, July 2008. Available at: http://www.clomedia.com/executive-briefings/2008/July/2262/index.php.

5. "Today's Tip Section," *BusinessWeek*, July 1, 2008.

6. "Why R. L. Polk & Co. is a Cool Place to Work." Available at: http://usa.polk .com/Careers/People/.

7. http://www.jobsataramco.com/eu/lifestyles.aspx.

8. www.kennedyinfo.com.

9. Much of this information comes from a conversation the author had with Nicole Bodem, Director, Search Marketing, Arbita - One World, Right Now.

10. http://careers.amd.com/en-us/culture_values.aspx.

11. www.gore.com.

12. Ross Clennett, "What a Journey!" ERE.net, September, 2008. Accessible at: http://www.ere.net/2008/09/24/what-a-journey/.

13. Ross Clennett, "What a Journey!" ERE.Net. Reprint permission from Ross Clennett to the author is on file with the author.

14. John L. White, *My JOB SUCKS and I CAN'T TAKE IT Anymore! HELP!: The Real-Life Job Survival Guide* (Zephyrhills, FL: Everlove and Bohannon Publishing, 2007).

15. Adapted from The EMERGE International Brand Scan.

Afterword

1. www.quantumpathic.com/.

2. Sherry Anshara, *The Age of Inheritance: The Activation of the 13 Chakras* (Scottsdale, AZ: QuantumPathic Press, 2004).

Appendix B

1. www.youtube.com/conwayinc.

2. Lizz Pellet and P.J. Bouchard, *Getting Your Shift Together: Making Sense of Organizational Culture and Change, Introducing Cultural Due Diligence,* (Cave Creek, AZ: CCI Press, 2000).

Index

About the Author

Lizz Pellet is the CEO of EMERGE International, a California-based consultancy firm dedicated to improving the ROI of organizational culture, employment branding, and transformational change efforts (www .emergeinternational.com). She is also a Fellow from Johns Hopkins University. She is the author of *Getting Your Shift Together: Making Sense of Organizational Culture* and *Change: Introducing Cultural Due Diligence*. Lizz is a member of the National Speakers Association and has presented more than 70 professional learning sessions in the past few years. She is a popular conference presenter, where participants enjoy her high energy, down-to-earth style, and humorous approach to culture, change, and transition.

PHOTO: AUDREY DEMPSEY, INFINITY PHOTO